BEYOND THE
PLEASURE
PRINCIPLE

By SIGMUND FREUD

THE STANDARD EDITION
OF THE COMPLETE PSYCHOLOGICAL WORKS OF
SIGMUND FREUD
24 VOLUMES

Sigmund Freud

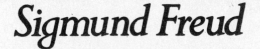

BEYOND THE
PLEASURE PRINCIPLE

TRANSLATED AND EDITED BY
James Strachey

INTRODUCTION BY
Gregory Zilboorg

WITH A BIOGRAPHICAL
INTRODUCTION BY
Peter Gay

W·W·NORTON & COMPANY
New York · London

Library of Congress Cataloging-in-Publication Data
Freud, Sigmund, 1856–1939
Beyond the pleasure principle.
Translation of Jenseits des Lust-Prinzips.
Reprint of the ed. published by Liveright, New York.
Bibliography: p.
Includes index.
1. Pleasure   2. Psychoanalysis.   I. Title.
BF173.F65   1975   150.19′52   74-22476

ISBN 0-393-00769-3

W. W. Norton & Company, Inc., is also the publisher of The Standard
Edition of the Complete Psychological Works of Sigmund Freud.

W. W. Norton & Company, Inc.
500 Fifth Avenue, New York, N.Y. 10110
www.wwnorton.com

W. W. Norton & Company Ltd.
Castle House, 75/76 Wells Street, London W1T 3QT

PRINTED IN THE UNITED STATES OF AMERICA

9 0

Contents

SIGMUND FREUD: A BRIEF LIFE

by *Peter Gay*

It was Freud's fate, as he observed not without pride, to "agitate the sleep of mankind." Half a century after his death, it seems clear that he succeeded far better than he expected, though in ways he would not have appreciated. It is commonplace but true that we all speak Freud now, correctly or not. We casually refer to oedipal conflicts and sibling rivalry, narcissism and Freudian slips. But before we can speak that way with authority, we must read his writings attentively. They repay reading, with dividends.

Sigmund Freud was born on May 6, 1856, in the small Moravian town of Freiberg.[1] His father, Jacob Freud, was an impecunious merchant; his mother, Amalia, was handsome, self-assertive, and young—twenty years her husband's junior and his third wife. Jacob Freud had two sons from his first marriage who were about Amalia Freud's age and lived nearby. One of these half brothers had a son, John, who, though Sigmund Freud's nephew, was older than his uncle.

---

[1]His given names were Sigismund Schlomo, but he never used his middle name and, after experimenting with the shorter form for some time, definitively adopted the first name Sigmund—on occasion relapsing into the original formulation—in the early 1870s, when he was a medical student at the University of Vienna. Freiberg, now in Czechoslovakia, bears the Czech name "Pribor."

Freud's family constellation, then, was intricate enough to puzzle the clever and inquisitive youngster. Inquisitiveness, the natural endowment of children, was particularly marked in him. Life would provide ample opportunity to satisfy it.

In 1860, when Freud was almost four, he moved with his family to Vienna, then a magnet for many immigrants. This was the opening phase of the Hapsburg Empire's liberal era. Jews, only recently freed from onerous taxes and humiliating restrictions on their property rights, professional choices, and religious practices, could realistically harbor hopes for economic advancement, political participation, and a measure of social acceptance. This was the time, Freud recalled, when "every industrious Jewish school boy carried a Cabinet Minister's portfolio in his satchel."[2] The young Freud was encouraged to cultivate high ambitions. As his mother's first-born and a family favorite, he secured, once his family could afford it, a room of his own. He showed marked gifts from his first school days, and in his secondary school, or Gymnasium, he was first in his class year after year.

In 1873, at seventeen, Freud entered the University of Vienna. He had planned to study law, but, driven on by what he called his "greed for knowledge," instead matriculated in the faculty of medicine, intending to embark, not on a conventional career as a physician, but on philosophical-scientific investigations that might solve some of the great riddles that fascinated him. He found his work in physiology and neurology so absorbing that he did not take his degree until 1881.

A brilliant researcher, he cultivated the habit of close observation and the congenial stance of scientific skepticism. He was privileged to work under professors with international reputations, almost all German imports and tough-

---

[2] *The Interpretation of Dreams* (1900), *SE* IV, 193.

minded positivists who disdained metaphysical speculations about, let alone pious explanations of, natural phenomena. Even after Freud modified their theories of the mind—in essence barely disguised physiological theories—he recalled his teachers with unfeigned gratitude. The most memorable of them, Ernst Brücke, an illustrious physiologist and a civilized but exacting taskmaster, confirmed Freud's bent as an unbeliever. Freud had grown up with no religious instruction at home, came to Vienna University as an atheist, and left it as an atheist—with persuasive scientific arguments.

In 1882, on Brücke's advice, Freud reluctantly left the laboratory to take a lowly post at the Vienna General Hospital. The reason was romantic: in April, he had met Martha Bernays, a slender, attractive young woman from northern Germany visiting one of his sisters, and fallen passionately in love. He was soon secretly engaged to her, but too poor to establish the respectable bourgeois household that he and his fiancée thought essential. It was not until September 1886, some five months after opening his practice in Vienna, with the aid of wedding gifts and loans from affluent friends, that the couple could marry. Within nine years, they had six children, the last of whom, Anna, grew up to be her father's confidante, secretary, nurse, disciple, and representative, and an eminent psychoanalyst in her own right.

Before his marriage, from October 1885 to February 1886, Freud worked in Paris with the celebrated French neurologist Jean-Martin Charcot, who impressed Freud with his bold advocacy of hypnosis as an instrument for healing medical disorders, and no less bold championship of the thesis (then quite unfashionable) that hysteria is an ailment to which men are susceptible no less than women. Charcot, an unrivaled observer, stimulated Freud's growing interest in the theoretical and therapeutic aspects of mental healing. Nervous ailments became Freud's specialty, and in the 1890s, as he told a friend, psychology became his tyrant. During these years he founded the psychoanalytic theory of mind.

He had intriguing if somewhat peculiar help. In 1887, he had met a nose-and-throat specialist from Berlin, Wilhelm Fliess, and rapidly established an intimate friendship with him. Fliess was the listener the lonely Freud craved: an intellectual gambler shocked at no idea, a propagator of provocative (at times fruitful) theories, an enthusiast who fed Freud ideas on which he could build. For over a decade, Fliess and Freud exchanged confidential letters and technical memoranda, meeting occasionally to explore their subversive notions. And Freud was propelled toward the discovery of psychoanalysis in his practice: his patients proved excellent teachers. He was increasingly specializing in women suffering from hysteria, and, observing their symptoms and listening to their complaints, he found that, though a good listener, he did not listen carefully enough. They had much to tell him.

In 1895, Freud and his fatherly friend Josef Breuer, a thriving, generous internist, published *Studies on Hysteria*, assigning Breuer's former patient "Anna O." pride of place. She had furnished fascinating material for intimate conversations between Breuer and Freud, and was to become, quite against her—and Breuer's—will, the founding patient of psychoanalysis. She demonstrated to Freud's satisfaction that hysteria originates in sexual malfunctioning and that symptoms can be talked away.

The year 1895 was decisive for Freud in other ways. In July, Freud managed to analyze a dream, his own, fully. He would employ this dream, known as "Irma's injection," as a model for psychoanalytic dream interpretation when he published it, some four years later, in his *Interpretation of*

Dreams. In the fall, he drafted, but neither completed nor published, what was later called the Project for a Scientific Psychology. It anticipated some of his fundamental theories yet serves as a reminder that Freud had been deeply enmeshed in the traditional physiological interpretation of mental events.

Increasingly Freud was offering psychological explanations for psychological phenomena. In the spring of 1896, he first used the fateful name, "psychoanalysis." Then in October his father died; "the most important event," he recalled a dozen years later, "the most poignant loss, of a man's life."[3] It supplied a powerful impetus toward psychoanalytic theorizing, stirring Freud to his unprecedented self-analysis, more systematic and thoroughgoing than the frankest autobiographer's self-probing. In the next three or four years, as he labored over his "Dream book," new discoveries crowded his days. But first he had to jettison the "seduction theory" he had championed for some time. It held that *every* neurosis results from premature sexual activity, mainly child molestation, in childhood.[4] Once freed from this farreaching but improbable theory, Freud could appreciate the share of fantasies in mental life, and discover the Oedipus complex, that universal family triangle.

Freud's *Interpretation of Dreams* was published in November 1899.[5] It treated all dreams as wish fulfillments, detailed the mental stratagems that translate their causes into the strange drama the awakening dreamer remembers,

---

[3]Ibid., xxvi.
[4]Freud never claimed that sexual abuse does not exist. He had patients who he knew had not imagined the assaults they reported. All he abandoned when he abandoned the seduction theory was the sweeping claim that *only* the rape of a child, whether a boy or a girl, by a servant, an older sibling, or a classmate, could be the cause of a neurosis.
[5]The book bears the date of 1900 on the title page and this date is usually given as the date of publication.

and, in the difficult seventh chapter, outlined a comprehensive theory of mind. Its first reception was cool. During six years, only 351 copies were sold; a second edition did not appear until 1909. However, Freud's popularly written *Psychopathology of Everyday Life* of 1901 found a wider audience. Its collection of appealing slips of all sorts made Freud's fundamental point that the mind, however disheveled it might appear, is governed by firm rules. Thus—to give but one typical instance—the presiding officer of the Austrian parliament, facing a disagreeable season, opened it with the formal declaration that it was hereby closed. That "accident" had been prompted by his hidden repugnance for the sessions ahead.

Gradually, though still considered a radical, Freud acquired prestige and supporters. He had quarreled with Fliess in 1900, and, though their correspondence lingered on for some time, the two men never met again. Yet in 1902, after unconscionable delays, apparently generated by anti-Semitism combined with distrust of the maverick innovator, he was finally appointed an associate professor at the University of Vienna. Late that year, Freud and four other Viennese physicians began meeting every Wednesday night in his apartment at Berggasse 19 to discuss psychoanalytic questions; four years after, the group, grown to over a dozen regular participants, employed a paid secretary (Otto Rank) to take minutes and keep records. Finally, in 1908, it was transformed into the Vienna Psychoanalytic Society. At least some medical men (and a few women) were taking Freud's ideas seriously.

In 1905, Freud buttressed the structure of psychoanalytic thought with the second pillar of his theory: the *Three Essays on the Theory of Sexuality*. It outlined perversions and "normal" development from childhood to puberty with a lack of censoriousness and an openness hitherto virtually unknown in medical literature. Again in 1905, Freud brought out his book on jokes and the first of his famous case histories: "Fragment of an Analysis of a Case of Hysteria," nicknamed the "Dora case." He published it to illustrate the uses of dream interpretation in psychoanalysis, and expose his failure to recognize the power of transference in the analytic situation, but its lack of empathy with his embattled teen-age analysand has made it controversial.

In the following decade, Freud enriched the technique of psychoanalysis with three more sophisticated case histories—"Analysis of a Phobia in a Five-Year-Old Boy" ("Little Hans"), "Notes upon a Case of Obsessional Neurosis" ("Rat Man") in 1909, and "Psycho-Analytic Notes on an Autobiographical Account of a Case of Paranoia" ("Schreber Case") in 1911. Despite recent reanalyses, they remain lucid expository models across a wide spectrum of mental ailments. Then, from 1910 on, Freud published pioneering, exceedingly influential papers on technique, to establish psychoanalytic method on sound foundations. Nor did he neglect theory; witness such an important paper as "Formulations on the Two Principles of Mental Functioning" (1911), in which he differentiated between the "primary process," the primitive, unconscious element in the mind, and the "secondary process," largely conscious and controlled.

During these years, Freud also broke out of the circumscribed bounds of clinical and theoretical specialization by publishing papers on religion, literature, sexual mores, biography, sculpture, prehistory, and much else. "Obsessive Actions and Religious Practices" (1907), "Creative Writers and Daydreaming" (1908), " 'Civilized' Sexual Morality and Modern Nervous Illness" (1908), and his widely debated study of the origins of homosexuality, "Leonardo da Vinci and a Memory of His Childhood" (1910), are only samples of his range. Freud took all of culture as his province. He was realizing the program he had outlined for himself in his youth: to solve some of the great riddles of human existence.

Yet Freud also found the decade from 1905 to 1914 agitating with the progress of, and disagreeable splits within, a rapidly emerging international movement—*his* movement. Psychoanalytic politics took center stage. Two principal sources of hope for the future of Freud's ideas, and later of envenomed contention, were the intelligent, Socialist Viennese physician Alfred Adler (1870–1937), and the original, self-willed Swiss psychiatrist Carl G. Jung (1875–1961). Adler had been among Freud's earliest adherents and remained for some years his most prominent Viennese advocate. But as professional interest in psychoanalysis—not all of it benevolent—grew apace, as Freud's upsetting ideas were being explored at psychiatrists' congresses, Freud aspired to enlarge the reach of psychoanalysis beyond its place of origin. Vienna, with its handful of followers, struck him as provincial, unsuitable as headquarters.

The first breakthrough came in 1906, when Jung, then principal psychiatrist at the renowned clinic Burghölzli in Zurich, sent Freud an offprint. Freud responded promptly; a cordial correspondence blossomed, and the friendship was cemented by Jung's visit to Freud in early 1907. Freud was only fifty, vigorous and productive, but he had long brooded on himself as aging and decrepit. He was seeking a successor who would carry the psychoanalytic dispensation to later generations and into a world larger than the Viennese, Jewish ambiance to which psychoanalysis was then confined. Jung, a formidable presence and energetic debater, was an inspired discovery: he was not old, he was not Viennese, he was not Jewish. Jung was prominent in the first international congress of psychoanalysts at Salzburg in the spring of 1908, and was appointed, the following year, editor of a newly

founded *Yearbook.* Freud, delighted with Jung, anointed
him his son, his crown prince—accolades that Jung welcomed, indeed encouraged. Hence, when the International
Psychoanalytic Association was founded in March 1910, in
Nürnberg, Jung was Freud's logical, inevitable, choice for
president. Freud's Viennese adherents saw their city displaced by Zurich as the center of psychoanalysis, and did not
like it. A compromise was hammered out, and for some time
peace reigned in the Vienna Psychoanalytic Society. But
Adler was developing distinctive psychological ideas, which
featured aggressiveness over sexuality, and "organ inferiority" as a dominant cause of neuroses. A split became inevitable, and, in the summer of 1911, Adler and some of his
adherents resigned, leaving Freud and the Freudians in control of the Vienna society.

Freud was not without accolades. In September 1909, he
had received an honorary doctorate at Clark University in
Worcester, Massachusetts, as had Jung. But like Adler, Jung
increasingly diverged from Freud's ideas. He had never been
easy with the prominence Freud assigned to the sexual
drive—libido. By early 1912, these reservations took a personal turn. In response, Ernest Jones, Freud's principal English lieutenant, formed a defensive secret band of like-
minded analysts, the Committee. It consisted of himself,
Freud, Sandor Ferenczi (a brilliant adherent from Budapest), the witty Viennese lawyer Hanns Sachs, the astute
Berlin clinician and theorist Karl Abraham, and Freud's
amanuensis, the autodidact Otto Rank. It seemed needed:
by late 1912, the correspondence between Jung and Freud
had grown acrimonious and in January 1914, Freud ter-
minated his friendship with Jung. A split was only a matter
of time; in the spring of 1914, Jung resigned from his powerful positions in the psychoanalytic movement.

The strains of psychoanalytic politics did not keep Freud

from continuing his explorations of an impressive variety of topics. In 1913, he published an audacious, highly speculative venture into psychoanalytic prehistory, *Totem and Taboo*, which specified the moment that savages, in some dim, remote past, entered culture by murdering their father and acquiring guilt feelings. Then, in 1914, he published (anonymously) "The Moses of Michelangelo," uniting his admiration for Michelangelo's brooding sculpture with his powers of observation. In the same year, with an unsettling paper on narcissism, he subverted crucial aspects of psychoanalytic thought by throwing doubts upon his theory of drives—hitherto divided into erotic and egoistic.

But harrowing events on the world stage shouldered aside Freud's reassessment of psychoanalytic theory. On June 28, 1914, Austria's Archduke Francis Ferdinand and his consort were assassinated. Six weeks later, on August 4, Europe was at war. The first casualty for psychoanalysis was Freud's eventually best-known case history, "From the History of an Infantile Neurosis" ("Wolf Man"), written in the fall of 1914, but not published until 1918. Psychoanalytic activity almost ground to a halt. Many potential patients were at the front; most psychoanalysts were drafted into the medical corps; communications between "enemies" like Ernest Jones and Freud were severely truncated; psychoanalytic publications almost vanished; and congresses, the lifeblood of communication, were out of the question. For Freud, these were anxious times in other ways: all three of his sons were in the army, two of them almost daily in mortal danger.

Yet the war did not idle Freud's mind. Having too much time on his hands, he used it to good purpose. Work was a defense against brooding. Between March and July 1915, he wrote a dozen fundamental papers on metapsychology—on the unconscious, on repression, on melancholia; but he refused to gather them into the basic textbook he had planned. He published five of the papers between 1915 and 1917, and destroyed the rest. His enigmatic dissatisfaction with them hints at the discontent that had fueled his paper on narcissism. His map of the mind was inadequate to the evidence he had accumulated in his clinical experience. But he still lacked a satisfactory alternative. That would have to wait until after the war.

Another wartime activity, though more successful, gave Freud only modest pleasure: beginning in 1915, he delivered lectures at the university, published as a single volume in 1917 as *Introductory Lectures on Psycho-Analysis.* With the cunning of the born popularizer, Freud opened with a series on ordinary experiences, slips of the tongue, "unmotivated" forgetting, then turned to dreams and concluded with the technical topic, neuroses. Frequently reprinted and widely translated, these *Introductory Lectures* finally secured Freud a wide audience.

The war dragged on. Originally, somewhat to his surprise, an Austrian patriot, Freud wearied of the endless slaughter. He grew appalled at the chauvinism of intellectuals, the callousness of commanders, the stupidity of politicians. He had not yet fully acknowledged the theoretical significance of aggression, even though psychoanalysts had regularly encountered aggressiveness among their patients. But the war, beastly as it was, confirmed the skeptical psychoanalytic appraisal of human nature.

Signs of revived activity came shortly before the end of hostilities. In September 1918, for the first time since 1913, psychoanalysts from Germany and Austria-Hungary met in Budapest. Two months later, the war was over. To the family's immense relief, all of Freud's sons survived it. But the time for worry was far from over. The defeated powers were faced with revolution, drastically transformed from empires into republics, and saddled with stringent, vindictive peace treaties stripping them of territory and resources. Vienna was hungry, cold, desperate; food and fuel shortages produced deadly ailments—tuberculosis and influenza. In this stressful situation, Freud, who wasted no tears on the departed Hapsburg Empire, proved an energetic, imaginative manager. The portrait of Martha Freud shielding Herr Professor from domestic realities needs revision. Freud dispatched precise requests abroad to relatives, friends, associates, specifying what nourishment and clothing his family needed most, and how to send packages safely. Then, in January 1920, postwar misery struck home with deadly force: Freud's beloved second daughter Sophie, married and living in Hamburg, mother of two children, died in the influenza epidemic.

It has been plausibly argued that her death suggested the pessimistic drive theory that Freud now developed. Actually, he had virtually completed *Beyond the Pleasure Principle* (1920), which first announced Freud's theory of the death drive, the year before. Once Freud had adopted this construct, in which the forces of life, Eros, dramatically confront the forces of death, Thanatos, he found himself unable to think any other way. In 1923, in his classic study *The Ego and the Id*, he completed his revisions. He now proposed a "structural theory" of the mind, which visualizes the mind as divided into three distinct yet interacting agencies: the id (the wholly unconscious domain of the mind, consisting of the drives and of material later repressed), the ego (which is partly conscious and contains the defense mechanisms and the capacities to calculate, reason, and plan), and the super-ego (also only partly conscious, which harbors the conscience and, beyond that, unconscious feelings of guilt). This new scheme did not lead Freud to abandon his classic characterization of mental activity—emphasizing the distance of thoughts from awareness—as either conscious, or preconscious, or wholly unconscious. But he now made the decisive point that many of the mental operations of the ego, and of the super-ego as well, are inaccessible to direct introspection.

Meanwhile, the psychoanalytic movement was flourishing. Freud was becoming a household word, though he detested the sensationalized attention the popular press gave him. Better: in 1920, at the first postwar congress at The Hague, former "enemies" met as friends. Freud was accompanied by his daughter Anna, whom he was then analyzing and who joined the Vienna Psychoanalytic Society in 1922. In that year, the analysts convened in Berlin. It was the last congress Freud ever attended. In April 1923, he was operated on for a growth in his palate. While for months his doctors and closest associates pretended that the growth was benign, by September the truth was out: he had cancer. Severe operations followed in the fall. From then on Freud, compelled to wear a prosthesis, was rarely free of discomfort or pain.

But he never stopped working. While he had trouble speaking, he continued to analyze patients, many of them American physicians who came to Vienna as his "pupils" and returned to analyze in New York or Chicago. He continued to revise his theories. From the mid-1920s on, he wrote controversial papers on female sexuality, and, in 1926, *Inhibitions, Symptoms, and Anxiety,* which reversed his earlier thinking on anxiety, now treating it as a danger signal. Moreover, he wrote essays that found a relatively wide public: *The Future of an Illusion,* a convinced atheist's dissection of religion, in 1927, and, in 1930, *Civilization and Its Discontents,* a disillusioned look at modern civilization on the verge of catastrophe.

In 1933, that catastrophe came. On January 30, Hitler was appointed chancellor in Germany, and from then on

Austrian Nazis, already active, increasingly intervened in politics. The old guard was disappearing: Karl Abraham had died prematurely in 1925; Sandor Ferenczi followed him in 1933. Freud's closest friends were gone. But Freud was unwilling to leave the Vienna he hated and loved: he was too old, he did not want to desert, and besides, the Nazis would never invade his country. On the morning of March 12, 1938, the Germans proved him wrong. As the Nazis marched in, a jubilant populace greeted them. Spontaneous anti-Semitic outrages surpassed anything Germans had witnessed after five years of Nazi rule. Late in March, Anna was summoned to Gestapo headquarters; while she was released unharmed, the trauma changed Freud's mind: he must emigrate. It took months to satisfy the Nazi government's extortions, but on June 4, Freud left for Paris, welcomed by his former analysand and loving disciple, Princess Marie Bonaparte. On June 6, Freud landed in London, preceded by most of his family, "to die in freedom."

Aged and ill, he kept on working. Freud's last completed book, *Moses and Monotheism,* irritated and dismayed his Jewish readers with its assertion that Moses had been an Egyptian: he ended life as he had lived it—a disturber of the peace. He died bravely on September 23, 1939, asking his physician for a lethal dose of morphine. Freud did not believe in personal immortality, but his work lives on.

ABOUT THIS BOOK

In the course of theorizing about psychoanalysis, Freud changed his mind on some important matters. Perhaps the most striking of these was his revision of drive—or, as the translators in the Standard Edition have it, instinct—theory. Before the First World War, Freud visualized the sexual confronting the egoistic drives. They were clearly distinct: the sexual drives were not egoistic, the egoistic drives not sexual; the first served the perpetuation of the species, the second the perpetuation of the self. But then, in his important paper "On Narcissism" (1914), Freud began to take a different line. There is, as he put it, an "ego-libido" just as there is an "object-libido," which is to say that the self, too, like other objects, can be erotically charged. But this meant that the old drive theory was no longer tenable. *Jenseits des Lustprinzips*, written in 1919 and published the following year, is the first clear statement of Freud's new drive theory. Love and life now stand over against aggression and death.

It has been suggested that Freud's new preoccupation with death as evidenced in *Beyond the Pleasure Principle* was the result of the death of Freud's charming daughter Sophie, who succumbed in the great influenza epidemic that took so many lives after the end of the First World War. But in fact, as Freud could easily document, he had written this little book while his Sophie was still enjoying perfect health. In short, *Beyond the Pleasure Principle,* an important theoretical revision of Freud's earlier ideas best read in conjunction with *The Ego and the Id* (1923), is not an exercise in autobiography but a turning point in psychoanalytic theory.

INTRODUCTION
by Gregory Zilboorg, M.D.

A question which seems natural and almost unavoidable arises: What can one say about a book, and a little one at that, which is forty years old, and which is supposedly not one of the most impressive or "spectacular" bits of Freud's many writings? The question presupposes the implied answer that forty years even in our swift-moving world is a long time, that the book in question is therefore more or less superannuated and deserves but a respectful historical glance before we put it back on the shelf to gather more dust.

It is obvious that the above is a rhetorical way of saying that forty years after its appearance and twenty years after Freud's death, *Beyond the Pleasure Principle* still deserves considerable attention, and that the reader would do well if he reads it with studious curiosity. Of recent years we have become so accustomed to the atmosphere of controversy which surrounds psychoanalysis and Freud that we have almost lost our capacity to pick up a book on psychoanalysis without wanting to know in advance whether the book is for or against it, or, if it is for it, whether it is for Freud or for Jung, or, if it is Freudian, whether it is orthodox or neo-Freudian. If we dared to be frank with ourselves, we would have no difficulty in admitting that our judgment of psycho-analysis is actually fragmentary and not too profound. We could also admit that some sort of partisanship possesses us, and that therefore we are preoccupied with "taking sides" long before we get acquainted with the very first elements of psychoanalysis and the many-sidedness of the subject.

It is because of the various prejudices which have inculcated themselves into psychoanalytical and nonpsychoanalytical circles that it is pertinent to invite both the initiated and the uninitiated reader to suspend his fragmentary judgment for a short while and re-read afresh the little book that is here offered, and acquaint or re-acquaint himself with the sound of Freud's written voice, with his way of saying things, and then with the substance of what he has to say.

An introduction is not supposed to explain in advance what is said in the book; still less is it meant to interpret it. Rather, it is intended to clarify some shadows and point to certain lights which will possibly set the book in a proper perspective.

Bearing this in mind, let us first recall that Freud wrote *Beyond the Pleasure Principle* when he was sixty-four years old—a mature age indeed—and at a time when psychoanalysis had already achieved considerable popularity, even though it was still possible to assess the degree of its importance by the number of enemies it had. The tone of the book, the mannerisms of its style are vigorous, poignant, almost controversial; Freud it seems was still combatting his opponents rather than trying to instruct his proponents. Almost to the last years of his life, Freud preserved this combative vigor of writing, and in *Beyond the Pleasure Principle* this aspect of style stands out markedly, particularly when he emphasizes his claim that he is a partisan of no special philosophy and that he is indifferent as to whether what he has to say does or does not fit any known philosophy.

This claim for independence is characteristic of Freud's personality and of all his writings, but I believe it in no way casts aspersion on his originality or his genius, if I say that this declaratory independence should not be taken too seriously. No one, and particularly no genius, is really free of the ideological inheritance which he carries within himself as a child of a given generation. He may not be aware of it, of course, but Freud would have been the last man in the world to equate not being aware of something with its nonexistence. For it was of course Freud himself who discovered and unfolded before us the staggering richness and power within us of so many things of which we are not aware.

It is of some interest in this connection to recall that Freud denied ever having been acquainted with the writings of Schopenhauer and Nietzsche before he formulated many of his ideas. It was beyond any doubt an honest denial. Yet it is a matter of record that Hitschmann, one of the earliest adherents of Freud, read a paper in Freud's house as early as 1905 (Freud being present, of course) on the very subject of Nietzsche's ideas as compared with some of Freud's theories. There is no doubt that, whether or not Freud ever read Nietzsche's *The Genealogy of Morals,* his was the temperament and the aspiration of a proud iconoclast who, to paraphrase an old saying of Maxim Gorki's, was born to soar and not to crawl, and for whom soaring accomplishment was not a pleasure in itself but a temporary level from which he strove to attain ever-greater heights.

If we cast but a glance at the rough sketch of a general psychology which we find in Freud's letters to Fliess, we cannot help but be struck by the depth, diapason and immense horizons which Freud envisaged as the culmination of his system. And these letters, we must remember, were written *before* 1900, that is to say, *before* the first book *(The Interpretation of Dreams)* which really launched psychoanalysis into the stormy waters of a world which never was able to approach the study of the psychology of man without prejudice and considerable animosity and controversy—be it religious, scientific, or plain pedestrian. The ambition with which Freud's mind was fired from the very outset, and his particular goal of discovering, or uncovering, the real nature of man's mind, predestined him as a thinker and a man to become a storm center for years to come.

He was also a daring paradox, giving the semblance of self-contradiction, of inconsistency, and of all-solidity. Freud's apparent readiness to change his mind added a great number of dissenters and detractors—as if the scientist who has the courage to change his mind about some of his own ideas has gained a point against himself. The great majority of people do confuse stubbornness for consistency, and rigidity of scientific ideas for soundness of position.

At any rate, *Beyond the Pleasure Principle* is one of the first great landmarks in Freud's ways of "changing his mind." I put these words in quotes to cast at least a little doubt on the traditional attitude that Freud did change his mind in this instance. He did not. What Freud did here was to add a path or two, a little curve or fork, in the tortuous intellectual road which he followed with dogged faith in his own intellectual independence. The additions or added trends of thought cannot be fully grasped and even less understood unless one always bears in mind the inner psychological atmosphere in which Freud worked in order to express his ideas.

His literary style was always terse, straightforward, clear and challengingly frank; but the same thing cannot be said about the emotional climate of his thought. First of all, Freud never gave up his belief—I am tempted to say faith— that the parallel he drew between Fechner's ideas in physics and his own in human psychology was not really a parallel but an actual proof that his concept of the mental apparatus and its energy was actually the same as Helmholtz' and Fechner's ideas about physical energy. To this faith he clung to the last, expressing the hope that some day the whole complexity of human reactions and relations could be reduced to some as yet undiscovered physico-chemical reactions. In other words, Freud remained an *organicist* throughout his scientific life. But genius and living paradox that he was, Freud was rejected by the materialists (conservative as well as Marxian) because of his alleged mysticism; and he was rejected by the idealists and religious thinkers because he was thought to be a materialist.

The contradictions into which Freud's detractors thus stumbled remained unnoticed as a rule, but Freud was of course aware of them and saw in them merely a sign of general resistance. Yet it was not only that. To Freud the epithet, "mystic," was an expression of opprobrium, and yet it was Freud who stated that saints were saved from severe neuroses by their sainthood, their faith; he mentioned in this connection St. Francis of Assisi. He who studies the lives of the saints would not easily issue to all of them, and without reservation, a certificate of psychological health. They were saints because they were able to stand the pressure of their respective neuroses rather than because they did not suffer from them. The lives of St. Ignatius Loyola, or San Francisco Xavier, or St. Augustine for that matter, offer ample confirmation of my viewpoint.

As one studies Freud, one can develop the strong suspicion that he was more attracted by many mystics than by physico-chemical hypotheses, and that he struggled with all the might of his great mind against openly giving in to the attraction of the mystical aspects of human life. In other words, the man who less than twenty years after he wrote *Beyond the Pleasure Principle* wrote his *Moses and Mono-*

theism, the man who some five years before *Beyond the Pleasure Principle* wrote the article on Michelangelo's *Moses,* seems throughout this span of time to have been preoccupied with the greatness of human intuitions and the universality of human strivings not only to solve but to participate in the mysteries of life. And it is perhaps because of this inclination that Freud gave signs of "protesting too much." (Perhaps too this is one of the reasons why his article on Michelangelo's *Moses* appeared first anonymously; it was only much later that it was admitted that Freud, the Editor-in-chief of the *Zeitschrift für Psychoanalyse,* was the real author of the article.)

While the complex question of Freud's intellectual struggles with his own ideas is far from solved, there is little doubt that the aggressive, trenchant, emphatic tone of his writings, which seem to be full of conviction and devoid of doubt, does not fully convey Freud's struggle with his own ideas, which at times must have reached heroic dimensions. It is because of Freud's aggressive candor, it seems to me, that his earliest followers seem more to have stood in awe, listening to his pronouncements, than actually to have assimilated his thought like true disciples, ready to ask friendly critical questions in order to deepen and broaden the understanding of their master's thought. The very few of his followers who were endowed with truly original minds and truly ambitious perspicacity and intuition soon broke with Freud; Jung is one of the few one can cite in this respect. The majority became either surly, hostile enemies—rather than scientific opponents—or admiring, enthusiastic followers—rather than scientific collaborators.

It is therefore of particular interest to note that there was hardly a psychoanalyst outside Freud himself who ever made an original contribution to the theory and practice of psychoanalysis; this is particularly true of the time when Freud wrote his *Beyond the Pleasure Principle.* The one exception one can cite with certainty was Karl Abraham, who made an inestimable contribution to the clinical understanding of character formation and of depression, a contribution which was spontaneously and "painlessly" incorporated into the body of psychoanalytic knowledge some five years before the appearance of *Beyond the Pleasure Principle.* But even in the case of Abraham things were not all clarity and sunshine; many of his colleagues were not very kindly disposed to the man, and Freud himself, as Jones has written, said that he was suspicious of his "Prussian mind"—Abraham being a Berliner.

All of the above amounts to saying that the constant and "true" followers of Freud were not very original minds; they were not mediocrities, but for some reason they would not or perhaps could not "speak up" until Freud spoke first. It is partly because of this that *Beyond the Pleasure Principle* acquired such significance in the history of the development of Freudian psychoanalysis. It acquired the reputation of a landmark in how Freud changed his mind and how daring he was in doing so. As a matter of cold fact, the book is an important contribution, a thrust forward in the growth of Freudian thought; but if one reads it carefully one will easily see that Freud *did not* change his mind, and that *Beyond the Pleasure Principle* did not overthrow any old psychoanalytic regime nor did it establish any new one. It was not even a small village revolution; it was and is a landmark of further development and a consolidation of the older pathways. *Beyond the Pleasure Principle* is what it says; it goes a little further beyond, but it does not abandon whatever preceded it.

This writer lays no claim to an understanding of Freud's writing better than anyone's else who approaches Freud with the earnestness he deserves and the tolerance which is imperative, even now some twenty years after Freud's death. I say "even now" for the following reason; at the beginning Freud had to suffer from the many whose quick and ever alert misjudgment of him multiplied by thousands the number of his antagonists in every walk of the world's intellectual life. Today, with the full text of Freud at the disposal of every curious reader of the world, everybody claims Freud as his own, because everybody just as alertly is ready to interpret Freud in his own way. Thus a plethora of "schools" has mushroomed in the psychological literature, each claiming its philosophical, moral and scientific right to consider Freud its *fons et origo,* and its own exclusive right to understand Freud in its own exclusively correct way. This splintering of interpreters and misinterpreters of Freud is not unnatural, of course; the process will undoubtedly continue for some time before the real Freud will stand out in the history of our intellectual development as a figure at whom and into whom we may look calmly and objectively.

Since it is not in anyone's power to slow down or to accelerate the salutary passage of time, it cannot be the ambition of this writer to attempt to do so. But this much it is legitimate for him to essay to do: to point out that the vigor of Freud's thought, stimulating as it has always been and is, is frequently obscured by his at times too hasty terminological innovations. Not that one objects to such innovations, or that one ought to insist on semantic hairsplitting; but Freud, whose clarity of thought and daring intellectual improvisations were always impressive and enlightening, suffered not infrequently from a certain confusion, at first unnoticeable but at length presenting an impediment to easy or clear understanding. *Beyond the Pleasure Principle* serves as an excellent example.

First, there is the tendency which imperceptibly grew

into assertive tradition that, having gone beyond the pleasure principle, he abandoned that principle. This, as I have already said, is not true. The reader, bearing this in mind, cannot fail but see it once the text is perused without prejudice, without the unwitting psychological twist which makes him read *Beyond the Pleasure Principle* and assume that the pleasure principle was left behind. We might as well state right here that the assiduous and faithful translators of Freud, in bringing before the English-speaking readers Freud's version of the pleasure-pain theory, did not help matters when they coined a neologism, "unpleasure." This awkward term is supposed to render somewhat accurately the German term *Unlust.* It is not an exactly successful rendition (except etymologically, perhaps). The feeling of pain, of discomfort, of that disagreeable malaise which Freud has in mind is not perceived as *un-*pleasure, for what we feel in this malaise we feel positively, and not negatively as a lack of something else. This point need not be labored; it is brought out here merely to illustrate how difficult it is to tell the reader what a given writer wants to say in a language his own, but not yours.

Now let us ask ourselves what appears to be new and not allegedly abandoned as old in *Beyond the Pleasure Principle.*

The concept of "compulsive repetition" or "repetition compulsion." Some still quarrel with this concept, some no longer do. The arguments for and against it are of no particular importance here. What is important is that new concepts, newly formulated, require greater clarity of definition. Freud discovered the repetitiveness of certain patterns of human behavior and the inevitability or, if you wish, the inescapable nature of this repetitiveness. And he called this phenomenon "repetition compulsion" or "compulsive repetition."

We have become accustomed to the term "compulsion" when we speak of compulsion neuroses—in other words, a neurosis which makes the sufferer therefrom *aware* that he is *"compelled* by something" to make this or that gesture or this or that turn or else he feels uncomfortable, uneasy, at times plainly anxious. It is hardly necessary to go into more detail to observe that the compulsive element of which Freud speaks when he speaks of compulsive repetition is something that the individual is *not* conscious of, that the compulsive element in this concept is something which is not neurotic at all, or not necessarily, and that it is just as or no more compulsive than breathing or the changing of the seasons. To use the term "compulsive" here connotes something that it is not and implies things which are not necessarily there—a rather strange semantic fuzziness on the part of that uniquely clear-minded thinker. Such unclarities are strewn throughout many of Freud's writings and translations, and if they do not always confuse the casual reader or even the student, one would do well in being forewarned and therefore in reading and studying Freud with considerable caution and prudence.

One more example: the second major innovation which Freud introduced into psychoanalytic thinking was the concept of the *death instinct.* Now we have become accustomed, particularly since Freud emphasized the role of instincts in the conscious and unconscious life of man, to consider an instinct a drive, an impulsive or perpetually compelling aspiration to gratify a *need.* In German, Freud uses the words *Trieb* and *Triebhaft,* which mean instinct, instinctual drive, a sense of being driven toward a certain even though not always comprehended goal. Under the circumstances, the term "death instinct" ought to mean an aspiration, a drive to be dead. Perhaps Freud was right, even though neither the biologist nor the theologian would find it possible to agree with him. Let us assume that Freud was right; he certainly did not prove his case, because there is nothing instinctual about dying, even though the end is inevitable. Here again we find a strange semantic or terminological confusion, a tendency to use terms which are familiar to us in the psychoanalytic glossaries, but which in certain contexts become somewhat confusing labels.

The above considerations may serve as a warning that it is not easy to understand great minds even when they appear to speak simply, or perhaps especially when their language appears simple and the terminology familiar.

EDITOR'S NOTE
Jenseits Des Lustprinzips

(a) GERMAN EDITIONS:

1920   Leipzig, Vienna and Zurich: Internationaler Psychoanalytischer Verlag. Pp. 60.

1921   2nd ed. Same publishers. Pp. 64.

1923   3rd ed. Same publishers. Pp. 94.

1925   *G.S.*, **6**, 191–257.

1931   *Theoretische Schriften*, 178–247.

1940   *G.W.*, **13**, 3–69.

(b) ENGLISH TRANSLATIONS:
Beyond the Pleasure Principle

1922   London and Vienna: International Psycho-Analytical Press. Pp. viii + 90. (Tr. C. J. M. Hubback; Pref. Ernest Jones.)

1924   New York: Boni and Liveright.

1942   London: Hogarth Press and Institute of Psycho-Analysis. (Re-issue of above.)

1950   Same Publishers. Pp. vi + 97. (Tr. J. Strachey.)

1955   *S.E.*, **18**, 3–64. (Modified version of above.)

Freud made a number of additions in the second edition, but subsequent alterations were negligible. The present translation is a corrected reprint of the *Standard Edition* version.

As is shown by his correspondence, Freud had begun working on a first draft of *Beyond the Pleasure Principle* in March, 1919, and he reported the draft as finished in the following May. During the same month he was completing his paper on 'The Uncanny' (1919*h*), which includes a paragraph setting out much of the gist of the present work in a few sentences. In this paragraph he refers to the 'compulsion to repeat' as a phenomenon exhibited in the behaviour of children and in psychoanalytic treatment; he suggests that this compulsion is something derived from the most intimate nature of the instincts; and he declares that it is powerful enough to disregard the pleasure principle. There is, however, no allusion to the 'death instincts'. He adds that he has already completed a detailed exposition of the subject. The paper on 'The Uncanny' containing this summary was published in the autumn of 1919. But Freud held back *Beyond the Pleasure Principle* for another year. In the early part of 1920 he was once more at work on it, and now, for the first time apparently, there is a reference to the 'death instincts' in a letter to Eitingon of February 20. He was still revising the work in May and June and it was finally completed by the middle of July, 1920. On September 9, he gave an address to the International Psycho-Analytical Congress at The Hague, with the title 'Supplements to the Theory of Dreams' *(Ergänzungen zur Traumlehre)*, in which he announced the approaching publication of the book; it was issued early in December. An 'author's abstract' of the address appeared in *Int. Z. Psychoanal.*, 6 (1920), 397–8. (A translation of this was published in *Int. J. Psycho-Anal.*, 1, 354.) It does not seem certain that this abstract was in fact by Freud himself, but it may be of interest to reprint it here (in a new translation).

'Supplements to the Theory of Dreams'

'The speaker dealt in his brief remarks with three points touching upon the theory of dreams. The first two of these were concerned with the thesis that dreams are wish-fulfilments and brought forward some necessary modifications of it. The third point related to material which brought complete confirmation of his rejection of the alleged "prospective" purposes of dreams.[1]

'The speaker explained that, alongside the familiar wishful dreams and the anxiety dreams which could easily be included in the theory, there were grounds for recognizing the existence of a third category, to which he gave the name of "punishment dreams". If we took into account the justifiable assumption of the existence of a special self-observing and critical agency in the ego (the ego ideal, the censor, conscience), these punishment dreams, too, should be subsumed under the theory of wish-fulfilment; for they would represent the fulfilment of a wish on the part of this critical agency. Such dreams, he said, had approximately the same relation to ordinary wishful dreams as the symptoms of obsessional neurosis, which arise from reaction formation, had to those of hysteria.

'Another class of dreams, however, seemed to the speaker to present a more serious exception to the rule that dreams are wish-fulfillments. These were the so-called "traumatic" dreams. They occur in patients suffering from accidents, but they also occur during psycho-analyses of neurotics and bring back to them forgotten traumas of childhood. In connection with the problem of fitting these dreams into the theory of wish-fulfillment, the speaker referred to a work

---

[1][See *The Interpretation of Dreams*, 1900a, VI (I), *Standard Ed.*, 5, 506–7 n.]

shortly to be published under the title of *Beyond the Plea-sure Principle.*

'The third point of the speaker's communication related to an investigation that had not yet been published, by Dr. Varendonck of Ghent. This author had succeeded in bring-ing under his conscious observation the production of un-conscious phantasies on an extensive scale in a half-sleeping state—a process which he described as "autistic thinking". It appeared from this enquiry that looking ahead at the possibilities of the next day, preparing attempts at solutions and adaptations, etc., lay wholly within the range of this preconscious activity, which also created latent dream-thoughts, and, as the speaker had always maintained, had nothing to do with the dream-work.'[2]

In the series of Freud's metapsychological writings, *Beyond the Pleasure Principle* may be regarded as introduc-ing the final phase of his views. He had already drawn attention to the 'compulsion to repeat' as a clinical phenom-enon, but here he attributes to it the characteristics of an instinct; here too for the first time he brings forward the new dichotomy between Eros and the death instincts which found its full elaboration in *The Ego and the Id* (1923*b*). In *Beyond the Pleasure Principle*, too, we can see signs of the new picture of the anatomical structure of the mind which was to dominate all Freud's later writings. Finally, the prob-lem of destructiveness, which played an ever more promi-nent part in his theoretical works, makes its first explicit appearance. The derivation of various elements in the pre-sent discussion from his earlier metapsychological works— such as 'The Two Principles of Mental Functioning'

---

[2]Cf. Freud's own preface to this book of Varendonck's (Freud, 1921*b*, *Standard Ed.*, 18, 271).

(1911*b*), 'Narcissism' (1914*c*) and 'Instincts and their Vicis-situdes' (1915*c*)—will be obvious. But what is particularly remarkable is the closeness with which some of the earlier sections of the present work follow the 'Project for a Scientific Psychology' (1950*a*), drafted by Freud twenty-five years earlier, in 1895.

Extracts from the earlier (1922) translation of this work were included in Rickman's *General Selection from the Works of Sigmund Freud* (1937, 162–194).

Editorial additions, whether to the text or the footnotes, are printed in square brackets.

BEYOND THE
PLEASURE
PRINCIPLE

I

In the theory of psycho-analysis we have no hesitation in assuming that the course taken by mental events is automatically regulated by the pleasure principle. We believe, that is to say, that the course of those events is invariably set in motion by an unpleasurable tension, and that it takes a direction such that its final outcome coincides with a lowering of that tension—that is, with an avoidance of unpleasure or a production of pleasure. In taking that course into account in our consideration of the mental processes which are the subject of our study, we are introducing an 'economic' point of view into our work; and if, in describing those processes, we try to estimate this 'economic' factor in addition to the 'topographical' and 'dynamic' ones, we shall, I think, be giving the most complete description of them of which we can at present conceive, and one which deserves to be distinguished by the term 'metapsychological'.[1]

It is of no concern to us in this connection to enquire how far, with this hypothesis of the pleasure principle, we have approached or adopted any particular, historically established, philosophical system. We have arrived at these speculative assumptions in an attempt to describe and to account

---

[1][See Section IV of 'The Unconscious' (1915e).]

for the facts of daily observation in our field of study. Priority
and originality are not among the aims that psycho-analytic
work sets itself; and the impressions that underlie the hypothesis of the pleasure principle are so obvious that they
can scarcely be overlooked. On the other hand we would
readily express our gratitude to any philosophical or psychological theory which was able to inform us of the meaning
of the feelings of pleasure and unpleasure which act so
imperatively upon us. But on this point we are, alas, offered
nothing to our purpose. This is the most obscure and inaccessible region of the mind, and, since we cannot avoid
contact with it, the least rigid hypothesis, it seems to me,
will be the best. We have decided to relate pleasure and
unpleasure to the quantity of excitation that is present in the
mind but is not in any way 'bound';[2] and to relate them in
such a manner that unpleasure corresponds to an *increase*
in the quantity of excitation and pleasure to a *diminution*.
What we are implying by this is not a simple relation between the strength of the feelings of pleasure and unpleasure
and the corresponding modifications in the quantity of excitation; least of all—in view of all we have been taught by
psycho-physiology—are we suggesting any directly propor-
tional ratio: the factor that determines the feeling is probably the amount of increase or diminution in the quantity of
excitation *in a given period of time.* Experiment might possibly play a part here; but it is not advisable for us analysts to
go into the problem further so long as our way is not pointed
by quite definite observations.[3]

---

[2][The concepts of 'quantity' and of 'bound' excitation, which run through
the whole of Freud's writings, found what is perhaps their most detailed
discussion in the early 'Project' (1950a [1895]). See in particular the long
discussion of the term 'bound' near the end of Section 1 of Part III of that
work. See also p. 28 f. below.]
[3][This point is again mentioned below on p. 57 and further developed in

We cannot, however, remain indifferent to the discovery that an investigator of such penetration as G. T. Fechner held a view on the subject of pleasure and unpleasure which coincides in all essentials with the one that has been forced upon us by psycho-analytic work. Fechner's statement is to be found contained in a small work, *Einige Ideen zur Schöpfungs- und Entwicklungsgeschichte der Organismen*, 1873 (Part XI, Supplement, 94), and reads as follows: 'In so far as conscious impulses always have some relation to pleasure or unpleasure, pleasure and unpleasure too can be regarded as having a psycho-physical relation to conditions of stability and instability. This provides a basis for a hypothesis into which I propose to enter in greater detail elsewhere. According to this hypothesis, every psycho-physical motion rising above the threshold of consciousness is attended by pleasure in proportion as, beyond a certain limit, it approximates to complete stability, and is attended by unpleasure in proportion as, beyond a certain limit, it deviates from complete stability; while between the two limits, which may be described as qualitative thresholds of pleasure and unpleasure, there is a certain margin of aesthetic indifference. . . .'[4]

The facts which have caused us to believe in the dominance of the pleasure principle in mental life also find expression in the hypothesis that the mental apparatus endeavours to keep the quantity of excitation present in it as low as possible or at least to keep it constant. This latter hypothesis is only another way of stating the pleasure principle; for if the work of the mental apparatus is directed towards keeping the quantity of excitation low, then anything that is calculated to increase that quantity is bound to

'The Economic Problem of Masochism' (1924*c*).]
[4] [Cf. 'Project', end of Section 8 of Part I.—'Aesthetic' is here used in the old sense of 'relating to sensation or perception'.]

be felt as adverse to the functioning of the apparatus, that is as unpleasurable. The pleasure principle follows from the principle of constancy: actually the latter principle was inferred from the facts which forced us to adopt the pleasure principle.[5] Moreover, a more detailed discussion will show that the tendency which we thus attribute to the mental apparatus is subsumed as a special case under Fechner's principle of the 'tendency towards stability', to which he has brought the feelings of pleasure and unpleasure into relation.

It must be pointed out, however, that strictly speaking it is incorrect to talk of the dominance of the pleasure principle over the course of mental processes. If such a dominance existed, the immense majority of our mental processes would have to be accompanied by pleasure or to lead to pleasure, whereas universal experience completely contradicts any such conclusion. The most that can be said, therefore, is that there exists in the mind a strong *tendency* towards the pleasure principle, but that that tendency is opposed by certain other forces or circumstances, so that the final outcome cannot always be in harmony with the tendency towards pleasure. We may compare what Fechner (1873, 90) remarks on a similar point: 'Since however a tendency towards an aim does not imply that the aim is attained, and

---

[5] [The 'principle of constancy' dates back to the very beginning of Freud's psychological studies. The first published discussion of it of any length was by Breuer (in semi-physiological terms) towards the end of Section 2(A) of his theoretical part of the *Studies on Hysteria* (Breuer and Freud, 1895). He there defines it as 'the tendency to keep intracerebral excitation constant'. In the same passage he attributes this principle to Freud and there in fact exist one or two earlier very brief references to it by Freud himself, though these were not published until after his death. (See Freud, 1941a [1892] and Breuer and Freud, 1940 [1892].) The subject is also discussed at length at the beginning of Freud's 'Project', under the name of 'neuronic inertia'.]

since in general the aim is attainable only by approxima-
tions. . . .'

If we turn now to the question of what circumstances are
able to prevent the pleasure principle from being carried
into effect, we find ourselves once more on secure and well-
trodden ground and, in framing our answer, we have at our
disposal a rich fund of analytic experience.

The first example of the pleasure principle being inhib-
ited in this way is a familiar one which occurs with regularity. We know that the pleasure principle is proper to a
primary method of working on the part of the mental apparatus, but that, from the point of view of the self-preservation of the organism among the difficulties of the external
world, it is from the very outset inefficient and even highly
dangerous. Under the influence of the ego's instincts of
self-preservation, the pleasure principle is replaced by the
reality principle. [6] This latter principle does not abandon the
intention of ultimately obtaining pleasure, but it nevertheless demands and carries into effect the postponement of
satisfaction, the abandonment of a number of possibilities
of gaining satisfaction and the temporary toleration of unpleasure as a step on the long indirect road to pleasure. The
pleasure principle long persists, however, as the method of
working employed by the sexual instincts, which are so hard
to 'educate', and, starting from those instincts, or in the ego
itself, it often succeeds in overcoming the reality principle,
to the detriment of the organism as a whole.

There can be no doubt, however, that the replacement of
the pleasure principle by the reality principle can only be
made responsible for a small number, and by no means the
most intense, of unpleasurable experiences. Another occa-

---

[6][See 'Formulations on the Two Principles of Mental Functioning', Freud
1911*b*.]

sion of the release of unpleasure, which occurs with no less
regularity, is to be found in the conflicts and dissensions that
take place in the mental apparatus while the ego is passing
through its development into more highly composite organizations. Almost all the energy with which the apparatus is
filled arises from its innate instinctual impulses. But these
are not all allowed to reach the same phases of development.
In the course of things it happens again and again that
individual instincts or parts of instincts turn out to be incompatible in their aims or demands with the remaining
ones, which are able to combine into the inclusive unity of
the ego. The former are then split off from this unity by the
process of repression, held back at lower levels of psychical
development and cut off, to begin with, from the possibility
of satisfaction. If they succeed subsequently, as can so easily
happen with repressed sexual instincts, in struggling
through, by roundabout paths, to a direct or to a substitutive
satisfaction, that event, which would in other cases have
been an opportunity for pleasure, is felt by the ego as unpleasure. As a consequence of the old conflict which ended
in repression, a new breach has occurred in the pleasure
principle at the very time when certain instincts were en-
deavoring, in accordance with the principle, to obtain fresh
pleasure. The details of the process by which repression
turns a possibility of pleasure into a source of unpleasure are
not yet clearly understood or cannot be clearly represented;
but there is no doubt that all neurotic unpleasure is of that
kind—pleasure that cannot be felt as such.[7]

The two sources of unpleasure which I have just indicated
are very far from covering the majority of our unpleasurable
experiences. But as regards the remainder it can be asserted

---

[7][*Footnote added* 1925:] No doubt the essential point is that pleasure and
unpleasure, being conscious feelings, are attached to the ego.

with some show of justification that their presence does not
contradict the dominance of the pleasure principle. Most of
the unpleasure that we experience is *perceptual* unpleasure.
It may be perception of pressure by unsatisfied instincts; or
it may be external perception which is either distressing in
itself or which excites unpleasurable expectations in the
mental apparatus—that is, which is recognized by it as a
'danger'. The reaction to these instinctual demands and
threats of danger, a reaction which constitutes the proper
activity of the mental apparatus, can then be directed in a
correct manner by the pleasure principle or the reality principle by which the former is modified. This does not seem
to necessitate any far-reaching limitation of the pleasure
principle. Nevertheless the investigation of the mental reaction to external danger is precisely in a position to produce
new material and raise fresh questions bearing upon our
present problem.

II

A condition has long been known and described which occurs after severe mechanical concussions, railway disasters and other accidents involving a risk to life; it has been given the name of 'traumatic neurosis'. The terrible war which has just ended gave rise to a great number of illnesses of this kind, but it at least put an end to the temptation to attribute the cause of the disorder to organic lesions of the nervous system brought about by mechanical force.[1] The symptomatic picture presented by traumatic neurosis approaches that of hysteria in the wealth of its similar motor symptoms, but surpasses it as a rule in its strongly marked signs of subjective ailment (in which it resembles hypochondria or melancholia) as well as in the evidence it gives of a far more comprehensive general enfeeblement and disturbance of the mental capacities. No complete explanation has yet been reached either of war neuroses or of the traumatic neuroses of peace. In the case of the war neuroses, the fact that the same symptoms sometimes came about without the intervention of any gross mechanical force seemed at once en-

---

[1] Cf. the discussion on the psycho-analysis of war neuroses by Freud, Ferenczi, Abraham, Simmel and Jones (1919) [to which Freud provided the introduction (1919d). See also his posthumously published 'Report on the Electrical Treatment of War Neuroses' (1955c [1920]).]

lightening and bewildering. In the case of the ordinary traumatic neuroses two characteristics emerge prominently:
first, that the chief weight in their causation seems to rest
upon the factor of surprise, of fright; and secondly, that a
wound or injury inflicted simultaneously works as a rule
against the development of a neurosis. 'Fright', 'fear' and
'anxiety'[2] are improperly used as synonymous expressions;
they are in fact capable of clear distinction in their relation
to danger. 'Anxiety' describes a particular state of expecting
the danger or preparing for it, even though it may be an
unknown one. 'Fear' requires a definite object of which to
be afraid. 'Fright', however, is the name we give to the state
a person gets into when he has run into danger without
being prepared for it; it emphasizes the factor of surprise. I
do not believe anxiety can produce a traumatic neurosis.
There is something about anxiety that protects its subject
against fright and so against fright-neuroses. We shall return
to this point later [p. 35 f.].[3]

The study of dreams may be considered the most trust-
worthy method of investigating deep mental processes. Now
dreams occurring in traumatic neuroses have the characteristic of repeatedly bringing the patient back into the situation of his accident, a situation from which he wakes up in
another fright. This astonishes people far too little. They
think the fact that the traumatic experience is constantly
forcing itself upon the patient even in his sleep is a proof of

---

[2] [In German, *'Schreck'*, *'Furcht'* and *'Angst'*.]
[3] [Freud is very far indeed from always carrying out the distinction he makes
here. More often than not he uses the word *'Angst'* to denote a state of
fear without any reference to the future. It seems not unlikely that in this
passage he is beginning to adumbrate the distinction drawn in *Inhibitions,
Symptoms and Anxiety* (1926d) between anxiety as a reaction to a traumatic situation—probably equivalent to what is here called *Schreck*—and
anxiety as a warning signal of the approach of such an event. See also his
use of the phrase 'preparedness for anxiety' on p. 25.]

the strength of that experience: the patient is, as one might say, fixated to his trauma. Fixations to the experience which started the illness have long been familiar to us in hysteria. Breuer and Freud declared in 1893[4] that 'hysterics suffer mainly from reminiscences'. In the war neuroses, too, observers like Ferenczi and Simmel have been able to explain certain motor symptoms by fixation to the moment at which the trauma occurred.

I am not aware, however, that patients suffering from traumatic neurosis are much occupied in their waking lives with memories of their accident. Perhaps they are more concerned with *not* thinking of it. Anyone who accepts it as something self-evident that their dreams should put them back at night into the situation that caused them to fall ill has misunderstood the nature of dreams. It would be more in harmony with their nature if they showed the patient pictures from his healthy past or of the cure for which he hopes. If we are not to be shaken in our belief in the wish-fulfilling tenor of dreams by the dreams of traumatic neurotics, we still have one resource open to us: we may argue that the function of dreaming, like so much else, is upset in this condition and diverted from its purposes, or we may be driven to reflect on the mysterious masochistic trends of the ego.[5]

At this point I propose to leave the dark and dismal subject of the traumatic neurosis and pass on to examine the method of working employed by the mental apparatus in one of its earliest *normal* activities—I mean in children's play.

---

[4] ['On the Psychical Mechanism of Hysterical Phenomena', end of Section I.]
[5] [The last 15 words of this sentence were added in 1921. For all this see *The Interpretation of Dreams* (1900a), *Standard Ed.*, 5, 550 ff.]

The different theories of children's play have only recently been summarized and discussed from the psychoanalytic point of view by Pfeifer (1919), to whose paper I would refer my readers. These theories attempt to discover the motives which lead children to play, but they fail to bring into the foreground the *economic* motive, the consideration of the yield of pleasure involved. Without wishing to include the whole field covered by these phenomena, I have been able, through a chance opportunity which presented itself, to throw some light upon the first game played by a little boy of one and a half and invented by himself. It was more than a mere fleeting observation, for I lived under the same roof as the child and his parents for some weeks, and it was some time before I discovered the meaning of the puzzling activity which he constantly repeated.

The child was not at all precocious in his intellectual development. At the age of one and a half he could say only a few comprehensible words; he could also make use of a number of sounds which expressed a meaning intelligible to those around him. He was, however, on good terms with his parents and their one servant-girl, and tributes were paid to his being a 'good boy'. He did not disturb his parents at night, he conscientiously obeyed orders not to touch certain things or go into certain rooms, and above all he never cried when his mother left him for a few hours. At the same time, he was greatly attached to his mother, who had not only fed him herself but had also looked after him without any outside help. This good little boy, however, had an occasional disturbing habit of taking any small objects he could get hold of and throwing them away from him into a corner, under the bed, and so on, so that hunting for his toys and picking them up was often quite a business. As he did this he gave vent to a loud, long-drawn-out 'o-o-o-o', accompanied by an expression of interest and satisfaction. His

mother and the writer of the present account were agreed
in thinking that this was not a mere interjection but represented the German word *'fort'* ['gone']. I eventually realized
that it was a game and that the only use he made of any of
his toys was to play 'gone' with them. One day I made an
observation which confirmed my view. The child had a
wooden reel with a piece of string tied round it. It never
occurred to him to pull it along the floor behind him, for
instance, and play at its being a carriage. What he did was
to hold the reel by the string and very skilfully throw it over
the edge of his curtained cot, so that it disappeared into it,
at the same time uttering his expressive 'o-o-o-o'. He then
pulled the reel out of the cot again by the string and hailed
its reappearance with a joyful *'da'* ['there']. This, then, was
the complete game—disappearance and return. As a rule
one only witnessed its first act, which was repeated untir-
ingly as a game in itself, though there is no doubt that the
greater pleasure was attached to the second act.[6]

The interpretation of the game then became obvious. It
was related to the child's great cultural achievement—the
instinctual renunciation (that is, the renunciation of instinctual satisfaction) which he had made in allowing his mother
to go away without protesting. He compensated himself for
this, as it were, by himself staging the disappearance and
return of the objects within his reach. It is of course a matter
of indifference from the point of view of judging the effec-

---

[6]A further observation subsequently confirmed this interpretation fully.
One day the child's mother had been away for several hours and on her
return was met with the words 'Baby o-o-o-o!' which was at first incompre-
hensible. It soon turned out, however, that during this long period of
solitude the child had found a method of making *himself* disappear. He had
discovered his reflection in a full-length mirror which did not quite reach
to the ground, so that by crouching down he could make his mirror-image
'gone'. [A further reference to this story will be found in *The Interpretation
of Dreams, Standard Ed.*, 5, 461 n.]

tive nature of the game whether the child invented it himself or took it over on some outside suggestion. Our interest is directed to another point. The child cannot possibly have felt his mother's departure as something agreeable or even indifferent. How then does his repetition of this distressing experience as a game fit in with the pleasure principle? It may perhaps be said in reply that her departure had to be enacted as a necessary preliminary to her joyful return, and that it was in the latter that lay the true purpose of the game. But against this must be counted the observed fact that the first act, that of departure, was staged as a game in itself and far more frequently than the episode in its entirety, with its pleasurable ending.

No certain decision can be reached from the analysis of a single case like this. On an unprejudiced view one gets an impression that the child turned his experience into a game from another motive. At the outset he was in a *passive* situation—he was overpowered by the experience; but, by repeating it, unpleasurable though it was, as a game, he took on an *active* part. These efforts might be put down to an instinct for mastery that was acting independently of whether the memory was in itself pleasurable or not. But still another interpretation may be attempted. Throwing away the object so that it was 'gone' might satisfy an impulse of the child's, which was suppressed in his actual life, to revenge himself on his mother for going away from him. In that case it would have a defiant meaning: 'All right, then, go away! I don't need you. I'm sending you away myself.' A year later, the same boy whom I had observed at his first game used to take a toy, if he was angry with it, and throw it on the floor, exclaiming: 'Go to the fwont!' He had heard at that time that his absent father was 'at the front', and was far from regretting his absence; on the contrary he made it quite clear that he had no desire to be disturbed in his sole possession of his mother.[7] We know of other children who liked to express similar hostile impulses by throwing away objects instead of persons.[8] We are therefore left in doubt as to whether the impulse to work over in the mind some overpowering experience so as to make oneself master of it can find expression as a primary event, and independently of the pleasure principle. For, in the case we have been discussing, the child may, after all, only have been able to repeat his unpleasant experience in play because the repetition carried along with it a yield of pleasure of another sort but none the less a direct one.

Nor shall we be helped in our hesitation between these two views by further considering children's play. It is clear that in their play children repeat everything that has made a great impression on them in real life, and that in doing so they abreact the strength of the impression and, as one might put it, make themselves master of the situation. But on the other hand it is obvious that all their play is influenced by a wish that dominates them the whole time— the wish to be grown-up and to be able to do what grown-up people do. It can also be observed that the unpleasurable nature of an experience does not always unsuit it for play. If the doctor looks down a child's throat or carries out some small operation on him, we may be quite sure that these frightening experiences will be the subject of the next game; but we must not in that connection overlook the fact that there is a yield of pleasure from another source. As the child passes over from the passivity of the experience to the activity of the game, he hands on the disagreeable experience to

---

[7]When this child was five and three-quarters, his mother died. Now that she was really 'gone' ('o-o-o'), the little boy showed no signs of grief. It is true that in the interval a second child had been born and had roused him to violent jealousy.

[8]Cf. my note on a childhood memory of Goethe's (1917*b*).

one of his playmates and in this way revenges himself on a substitute.

Nevertheless, it emerges from this discussion that there is no need to assume the existence of a special imitative instinct in order to provide a motive for play. Finally, a reminder may be added that the artistic play and artistic imitation carried out by adults, which, unlike children's, are aimed at an audience, do not spare the spectators (for instance, in tragedy) the most painful experiences and can yet be felt by them as highly enjoyable.[9] This is convincing proof that, even under the dominance of the pleasure principle, there are ways and means enough of making what is in itself unpleasurable into a subject to be recollected and worked over in the mind. The consideration of these cases and situations, which have a yield of pleasure as their final outcome, should be undertaken by some system of aesthetics with an economic approach to its subject-matter. They are of no use for *our* purposes, since they presuppose the existence and dominance of the pleasure principle; they give no evidence of the operation of tendencies *beyond* the pleasure principle, that is, of tendencies more primitive than it and independent of it.

---

[9][Freud had made a tentative study of this point in his posthumously published paper on 'Psychopathic Characters on the Stage' (1942a) which was probably written in 1905 or 1906.]

III

Twenty-five years of intense work have had as their result that the immediate aims of psycho-analytic technique are quite other to-day than they were at the outset. At first the analysing physician could do no more than discover the unconscious material that was concealed from the patient, put it together, and, at the right moment, communicate it to him. Psycho-analysis was then first and foremost an art of interpreting. Since this did not solve the therapeutic problem, a further aim quickly came in view: to oblige the patient to confirm the analyst's construction from his own memory. In that endeavour the chief emphasis lay upon the patient's resistances: the art consisted now in uncovering these as quickly as possible, in pointing them out to the patient and in inducing him by human influence—this was where suggestion operating as 'transference' played its part—to abandon his resistances.

But it became ever clearer that the aim which had been set up—the aim that what was unconscious should become conscious—is not completely attainable by that method. The patient cannot remember the whole of what is repressed in him, and what he cannot remember may be precisely the essential part of it. Thus he acquires no sense of conviction of the correctness of the construction that has been communicated to him. He is obliged to *repeat* the repressed material as a contemporary experience instead of, as the physician would prefer to see, *remembering* it as something belonging to the past.[1] These reproductions, which emerge with such unwished-for exactitude, always have as their subject some portion of infantile sexual life—of the Oedipus complex, that is, and its derivatives; and they are invariably acted out in the sphere of the transference, of the patient's relation to the physician. When things have reached this stage, it may be said that the earlier neurosis has now been replaced by a fresh, 'transference neurosis'. It has been the physician's endeavour to keep this transference neurosis within the narrowest limits: to force as much as possible into the channel of memory and to allow as little as possible to emerge as repetition. The ratio between what is remembered and what is reproduced varies from case to case. The physician cannot as a rule spare his patient this phase of the treatment. He must get him to re-experience some portion of his forgotten life, but must see to it, on the other hand, that the patient retains some degree of aloofness, which will enable him, in spite of everything, to recognize that what appears to be reality is in fact only a reflection of a forgotten past. If this can be successfully achieved, the patient's sense of conviction is won, together with the therapeutic success that is dependent on it.

In order to make it easier to understand this 'compulsion

---

[1]See my paper on 'Recollecting, Repeating and Working Through' (1914*g*). [An early reference will be found in this same paper to the 'compulsion to repeat', which is one of the principle topics discussed in the present work. (See also the Editor's Note above, p. *xxxvii.*)—The term 'transference neurosis' in the special sense in which it is used a few lines lower down also appears in that paper.]

to repeat', which emerges during the psycho-analytic treatment of neurotics, we must above all get rid of the mistaken notion that what we are dealing with in our struggle against resistances is resistance on the part of the *unconscious*. The unconscious—that is to say, the 'repressed'—offers no resistance whatever to the efforts of the treatment. Indeed, it itself has no other endeavour than to break through the pressure weighing down on it and force its way either to consciousness or to a discharge through some real action. Resistance during treatment arises from the same higher strata and systems of the mind which originally carried out repression. But the fact that, as we know from experience, the motives of the resistances, and indeed the resistances themselves, are unconscious at first during the treatment, is a hint to us that we should correct a shortcoming in our terminology. We shall avoid a lack of clarity if we make our contrast not between the conscious and the unconscious but between the coherent *ego*[2] and the *repressed*. It is certain that much of the ego is itself unconscious, and notably what we may describe as its nucleus;[3] only a small part of it is covered by the term 'preconscious'.[4] Having replaced a purely descriptive terminology by one which is systematic or dynamic, we can say that the patient's resistance arises from his ego,[5] and we then at once perceive that the compulsion to repeat must be ascribed to the unconscious repressed. It seems probable that the compulsion can only express itself

---

[2][Cf. a discussion of this in the Editor's Introduction to *The Ego and the Id* (1923*b*), *Standard Ed.*, 19, 7–8; *I.P.L.*, 12, xiii–xiv.]

[3][This is corrected in a footnote at the beginning of Chapter III of *The Ego and the Id*, ibid., 28, and ibid., 16.]

[4][In its present form this sentence dates from 1921. In the first edition (1920) it ran: 'It may be that much of the ego is itself unconscious; only a part of it, probably, is covered by the term "preconscious".']

[5][A fuller and somewhat different account of the sources of resistance will be found in Chap. XI of *Inhibitions, Symptoms and Anxiety* (1926*d*).]

after the work of treatment has gone half-way to meet it and has loosened the repression.[6]

There is no doubt that the resistance of the conscious and unconscious ego operates under the sway of the pleasure principle: it seeks to avoid the unpleasure which would be produced by the liberation of the repressed. *Our* efforts, on the other hand, are directed towards procuring the toleration of that unpleasure by an appeal to the reality principle. But how is the compulsion to repeat—the manifestation of the power of the repressed—related to the pleasure principle? It is clear that the greater part of what is re-experienced under the compulsion to repeat must cause the ego unpleasure, since it brings to light activities of repressed instinctual impulses. That, however, is unpleasure of a kind we have already considered and does not contradict the pleasure principle: unpleasure for one system and simultaneously satisfaction for the other.[7] But we come now to a new and remarkable fact, namely that the compulsion to repeat also recalls from the past experiences which include no possibility of pleasure, and which can never, even long ago, have brought satisfaction even to instinctual impulses which have since been repressed.

The early efflorescence of infantile sexual life is doomed to extinction because its wishes are incompatible with reality and with the inadequate stage of development which the child has reached. That efflorescence comes to an end in the most distressing circumstances and to the accompaniment of the most painful feelings. Loss of love and failure leave

---

[6][*Footnote added* 1923:] I have argued elsewhere [1923c] that what thus comes to the help of the compulsion to repeat is the factor of 'suggestion' in the treatment—that is, the patient's submissiveness to the physician, which has its roots deep in his unconscious parental complex.

[7][Cf. Freud's allegorical use of the fairy tale of the 'Three Wishes' at the beginning of Lecture XIV of his *Introductory Lectures* (1916–17).]

behind them a permanent injury to self-regard in the form of a narcissistic scar, which in my opinion, as well as in Marcinowski's (1918), contributes more than anything to the 'sense of inferiority' which is so common in neurotics. The child's sexual researches, on which limits are imposed by his physical development, lead to no satisfactory conclusion; hence such later complaints as 'I can't accomplish anything; I can't succeed in anything'. The tie of affection, which binds the child as a rule to the parent of the opposite sex, succumbs to disappointment, to a vain expectation of satisfaction or to jealousy over the birth of a new baby—unmistakable proof of the infidelity of the object of the child's affections. His own attempt to make a baby himself, carried out with tragic seriousness, fails shamefully. The lessening amount of affection he receives, the increasing demands of education, hard words and an occasional punishment—these show him at last the full extent to which he has been scorned. These are a few typical and constantly recurring instances of the ways in which the love characteristic of the age of childhood is brought to a conclusion.

Patients repeat all of these unwanted situations and painful emotions in the transference and revive them with the greatest ingenuity. They seek to bring about the interruption of the treatment while it is still incomplete; they contrive once more to feel themselves scorned, to oblige the physician to speak severely to them and treat them coldly; they discover appropriate objects for their jealousy; instead of the passionately desired baby of their childhood, they produce a plan or a promise of some grand present—which turns out as a rule to be no less unreal. None of these things can have produced pleasure in the past, and it might be supposed that they would cause less unpleasure to-day if they emerged as memories or dreams instead of taking the form of fresh experiences. They are of course the activities of instincts intended to lead to satisfaction; but no lesson has been learnt from the old experience of these activities having led instead only to unpleasure.[8] In spite of that, they are repeated, under pressure of a compulsion.

What psycho-analysis reveals in the transference phenomena of neurotics can also be observed in the lives of some normal people. The impression they give is of being pursued by a malignant fate or possessed by some 'daemonic' power; but psycho-analysis has always taken the view that their fate is for the most part arranged by themselves and determined by early infantile influences. The compulsion which is here in evidence differs in no way from the compulsion to repeat which we have found in neurotics, even though the people we are now considering have never shown any signs of dealing with a neurotic conflict by producing symptoms. Thus we have come across people all of whose human relationships have the same outcome: such as the benefactor who is abandoned in anger after a time by each of his *protégés*, however much they may otherwise differ from one another, and who thus seems doomed to taste all the bitterness of ingratitude; or the man who friendships all end in betrayal by his friend; or the man who time after time in the course of his life raises someone else into a position of great private or public authority and then, after a certain interval, himself upsets that authority and replaces him by a new one; or, again, the lover each of whose love affairs with a woman passes through the same phases and reaches the same conclusion. This 'perpetual recurrence of the same thing' causes us no astonishment when it relates to *active* behaviour on the part of the person concerned and when we can discern in him an essential character-trait which always remains the same and which is compelled to

---

[8][This sentence was added in 1921.]

find expression in a repetition of the same experiences. We are much more impressed by cases where the subject appears to have a *passive* experience, over which he has no influence, but in which he meets with a repetition of the same fatality. There is the case, for instance, of the woman who married three successive husbands each of whom fell ill soon afterwards and had to be nursed by her on their death-beds.[9] The most moving poetic picture of a fate such as this is given by Tasso in his romantic epic *Gerusalemme Liberata*. Its hero, Tancred, unwittingly kills his beloved Clorinda in a duel while she is disguised in the armour of an enemy knight. After her burial he makes his way into a strange magic forest which strikes the Crusaders' army with terror. He slashes with his sword at a tall tree; but blood streams from the cut and the voice of Clorinda, whose soul is imprisoned in the tree, is heard complaining that he has wounded his beloved once again.

If we take into account observations such as these, based upon behaviour in the transference and upon the life-histories of men and women, we shall find courage to assume that there really does exist in the mind a compulsion to repeat which overrides the pleasure principle. Now too we shall be inclined to relate to this compulsion the dreams which occur in traumatic neuroses and the impulse which leads children to play.

But it is to be noted that only in rare instances can we observe the pure effects of the compulsion to repeat, unsupported by other motives. In the case of children's play we have already laid stress on the other ways in which the emergence of the compulsion may be interpreted; the compulsion to repeat and instinctual satisfaction which is immediately pleasurable seem to converge here into an intimate

---

[9] Cf. the apt remarks on this subject by C. G. Jung (1909).

partnership. The phenomena of transference are obviously exploited by the resistance which the ego maintains in its pertinacious insistence upon repression; the compulsion to repeat, which the treatment tries to bring into its service is, as it were, drawn over by the ego to *its* side (clinging as the ego does to the pleasure principle).[10] A great deal of what might be described as the compulsion of destiny seems intelligible on a rational basis; so that we are under no necessity to call in a new and mysterious motive force to explain it.

The least dubious instance [of such a motive force] is perhaps that of traumatic dreams. But on maturer reflection we shall be forced to admit that even in the other instances the whole ground is not covered by the operation of the familiar motive forces. Enough is left unexplained to justify the hypothesis of a compulsion to repeat—something that seems more primitive, more elementary, more instinctual than the pleasure principle which it over-rides. But if a compulsion to repeat *does* operate in the mind, we should be glad to know something about it, to learn what function it corresponds to, under what conditions it can emerge and what its relation is to the pleasure principle—to which, after all, we have hitherto ascribed dominance over the course of the processes of excitation in mental life.

---

[10][Before 1923 the last clause read: 'the compulsion to repeat is as it were called to its help by the ego, clinging as it does to the pleasure principle.']

IV

What follows is speculation, often far-fetched speculation, which the reader will consider or dismiss according to his individual predilection. It is further an attempt to follow out an idea consistently, out of curiosity to see where it will lead.

Psycho-analytic speculation takes as its point of departure the impression, derived from examining unconscious processes, that consciousness may be, not the most universal attribute of mental processes, but only a particular function of them. Speaking in metapsychological terms, it asserts that consciousness is a function of a particular system which it describes as *Cs.*[1] What consciousness yields consists essentially of perceptions of excitations coming from the external world and of feelings of pleasure and unpleasure which can only arise from within the mental apparatus; it is therefore possible to assign to the system *Pcpt.-Cs.*[2] a position in space. It must lie on the borderline between outside and inside; it must be turned towards the external world and must envelop the other psychical systems. It will be seen

---

[1] [See Freud, *The Interpretation of Dreams* (1900a), *Standard Ed.*, 5, 610 ff., and 'The Unconscious' (1915e), Section II.]

[2] [The system *Pcpt.* (the perceptual system) was first described by Freud in *The Interpretation of Dreams*, *Standard Ed.*, 5, 536 ff. In a later paper (1917d) he argued that the system *Pcpt.* coincided with the system *Cs.*]

that there is nothing daringly new in these assumptions; we have merely adopted the views on localization held by cerebral anatomy, which locates the 'seat' of consciousness in the cerebral cortex—the outermost, enveloping layer of the central organ. Cerebral anatomy has no need to consider why, speaking anatomically, consciousness should be lodged on the surface of the brain instead of being safely housed somewhere in its inmost interior. Perhaps *we* shall be more successful in accounting for this situation in the case of our system *Pcpt.-Cs.*

Consciousness is not the only distinctive character which we ascribe to the processes in that system. On the basis of impressions derived from our psycho-analytic experience, we assume that all excitatory processes that occur in the *other* systems leave permanent traces behind in them which form the foundation of memory. Such memory-traces, then, have nothing to do with the fact of becoming conscious; indeed they are often most powerful and most enduring when the process which left them behind was one which never entered consciousness. We find it hard to believe, however, that permanent traces of excitation such as these are also left in the system *Pcpt.-Cs.* If they remained constantly conscious, they would very soon set limits to the system's aptitude for receiving fresh excitations.[3] If, on the other hand, they were unconscious, we should be faced with the problem of explaining the existence of unconscious processes in a system whose functioning was otherwise accompanied by the phenomenon of consciousness. We should, so to say,

---

[3] What follows is based throughout on Breuer's views in [the second section of his theoretical contribution to] *Studies on Hysteria* (Breuer and Freud, 1895). [Freud himself discussed the subject in *The Interpretation of Dreams, Standard Ed.*, 5, 538 and it had previously been fully considered in his 'Project' of 1895 (1950a), Part I, Section 3. He returned to the topic later in his paper on the 'Mystic Writing-Pad' (1925a).]

have altered nothing and gained nothing by our hypothesis
relegating the process of becoming conscious to a special
system. Though this consideration is not absolutely conclusive, it nevertheless leads us to suspect that becoming conscious and leaving behind a memory-trace are processes incompatible with each other within one and the same system.
Thus we should be able to say that the excitatory process
becomes conscious in the system *Cs.* but leaves no permanent trace behind there; but that the excitation is transmitted to the systems lying next within and that it is in *them*
that its traces are left. I followed these same lines in the
schematic picture which I included in the speculative section of my *Interpretation of Dreams.* [4] It must be borne in
mind that little enough is known from other sources of the
origin of consciousness; when, therefore, we lay down the
proposition that *consciousness arises instead of a memory-
trace,* the assertion deserves consideration, at all events on
the ground of its being framed in fairly precise terms.

If this is so, then, the system *Cs.* is characterized by the
peculiarity that in it (in contrast to what happens in the
other psychical systems) excitatory processes do not leave
behind any permanent change in its elements but expire, as
it were, in the phenomenon of becoming conscious. An
exception of this sort to the general rule requires to be
explained by some factor that applies exclusively to that one
system. Such a factor, which is absent in the other systems,
might well be the exposed situation of the system *Cs.*,
immediately abutting as it does on the external world.

Let us picture a living organism in its most simplified
possible form as an undifferentiated vesicle of a substance
that is susceptible to stimulation. Then the surface turned
towards the external world will from its very situation be

---

[4] [*Standard Ed.,* 5, 538.]

differentiated and will serve as an organ for receiving stimuli. Indeed embryology, in its capacity as a recapitulation of developmental history, actually shows us that the central nervous system originates from the ectoderm; the grey matter of the cortex remains a derivative of the primitive superficial layer of the organism and may have inherited some of its essential properties. It would be easy to suppose, then, that as a result of the ceaseless impact of external stimuli on the surface of the vesicle, its substance to a certain depth may have become permanently modified, so that excitatory processes run a different course in it from what they run in the deeper layers. A crust would thus be formed which would at last have been so thoroughly 'baked through' by stimulation that it would present the most favourable possible conditions for the reception of stimuli and become incapable of any further modification. In terms of the system *Cs.*, this would mean that its elements could undergo no further permanent modification from the passage of excitation, because they had already been modified in the respect in question to the greatest possible extent: now, however, they would have become capable of giving rise to consciousness. Various ideas may be formed which cannot at present be verified as to the nature of this modification of the substance and of the excitatory process. It may be supposed that, in passing from one element to another, an excitation has to overcome a resistance, and that the diminution of resistance thus effected is what lays down a permanent trace of the excitation, that is, a facilitation. In the system *Cs.*, then, resistance of this kind to passage from one element to another would no longer exist.[5] This picture can be brought into relation with Breuer's distinction between quiescent (or

[5][This passage is foreshadowed in the later half of Section 3 of Part I of the 'Project'.]

bound) and mobile cathectic energy in the elements of the psychical systems;[6] the elements of the system *Cs.* would carry no bound energy but only energy capable of free discharge. It seems best, however, to express oneself as cautiously as possible on these points. None the less, this speculation will have enabled us to bring the origin of consciousness into some sort of connection with the situation of the system *Cs.* and with the peculiarities that must be ascribed to the excitatory processes taking place in it.

But we have more to say of the living vesicle with its receptive cortical layer. This little fragment of living substance is suspended in the middle of an external world charged with the most powerful energies; and it would be killed by the stimulation emanating from these if it were not provided with a protective shield against stimuli. It acquires the shield in this way: its outermost surface ceases to have the structure proper to living matter, becomes to some degree inorganic and thenceforward functions as a special envelope or membrane resistant to stimuli. In consequence, the energies of the external world are able to pass into the next underlying layers, which have remained living, with only a fragment of their original intensity; and these layers can devote themselves, behind the protective shield, to the reception of the amounts of stimulus which have been allowed through it. By its death, the outer layer has saved all the deeper ones from a similar fate—unless, that is to say, stimuli reach it which are so strong that they break through the protective shield. *Protection against* stimuli is an almost more important function for the living organism than *reception of* stimuli. The protective shield is supplied with its own

---

[6]Breuer and Freud, 1895. [See Section 2 of Breuer's theoretical contribution, and in particular the footnote at the beginning of that section. Cf. also footnote 1 on p. 2 above.]

store of energy and must above all endeavour to preserve the special modes of transformation of energy operating in it against the effects threatened by the enormous energies at work in the external world—effects which tend towards a levelling out of them and hence towards destruction. The main purpose of the *reception* of stimuli is to discover the direction and nature of the external stimuli; and for that it is enough to take small specimens of the external world, to sample it in small quantities. In highly developed organisms the receptive cortical layer of the former vesicle has long been withdrawn into the depths of the interior of the body, though portions of it have been left behind on the surface immediately beneath the general shield against stimuli. These are the sense organs, which consist essentially of apparatus for the reception of certain specific effects of stimulation, but which also include special arrangements for further protection against excessive amounts of stimulation and for excluding unsuitable kinds of stimuli.[7] It is characteristic of them that they deal only with very small quantities of external stimulation and only take in *samples* of the external world. They may perhaps be compared with feelers which are all the time making tentative advances towards the external world and then drawing back from it.

At this point I shall venture to touch for a moment upon a subject which would merit the most exhaustive treatment. As a result of certain psycho-analytic discoveries, we are to-day in a position to embark on a discussion of the Kantian theorem that time and space are 'necessary forms of thought'. We have learnt that unconscious mental processes are in themselves 'timeless'.[8] This means in the first place that they are not ordered temporally, that time does not

---

[7][Cf. 'Project', Part I, Sections 5 and 9.]
[8][See Section V of 'The Unconscious' (1915e).]

change them in any way and that the idea of time cannot
be applied to them. These are negative characteristics which
can only be clearly understood if a comparison is made with
conscious mental processes. On the other hand, our abstract
idea of time seems to be wholly derived from the method
of working of the system *Pcpt.-Cs.* and to correspond to a
perception on its own part of that method of working. This
mode of functioning may perhaps constitute another way of
providing a shield against stimuli. I know that these remarks
must sound very obscure, but I must limit myself to these
hints.[9]

We have pointed out how the living vesicle is provided
with a shield against stimuli from the external world; and we
had previously shown that the cortical layer next to that
shield must be differentiated as an organ for receiving stimuli from without. This sensitive cortex, however, which is
later to become the system *Cs.*, also receives excitations
from *within*. The situation of the system between the outside and the inside and the difference between the conditions governing the reception of excitations in the two cases
have a decisive effect on the functioning of the system and
of the whole mental apparatus. Towards the outside it is
shielded against stimuli, and the amounts of excitation im-
pinging on it have only a reduced effect. Towards the inside
there can be no such shield;[10] the excitations in the deeper
layers extend into the system directly and in undiminished
amount, in so far as certain of their characteristics give rise
to feelings in the pleasure-unpleasure series. The excitations
coming from within are, however, in their intensity and in
other, qualitative, respects—in their amplitude, perhaps—

---

[9][Freud recurs to the origin of the idea of time at the end of his paper on
'The Mystic Writing-Pad' (1925a). The same paper contains a further
discussion of the 'shield against stimuli'.]

[10][Cf. 'Project', beginning of Section 10 of Part I.]

more commensurate with the system's method of working than the stimuli which stream in from the external world.[11] This state of things produces two definite results. First, the feelings of pleasure and unpleasure (which are an index to what is happening in the interior of the apparatus) predominate over all external stimuli. And secondly, a particular way is adopted of dealing with any internal excitations which produce too great an increase of unpleasure: there is a tendency to treat them as though they were acting, not from the inside, but from the outside, so that it may be possible to bring the shield against stimuli into operation as a means of defence against them. This is the origin of *projection,* which is destined to play such a large part in the causation of pathological processes.

I have an impression that these last considerations have brought us to a better understanding of the dominance of the pleasure principle; but no light has yet been thrown on the cases that contradict that dominance. Let us therefore go a step further. We describe as 'traumatic' any excitations from outside which are powerful enough to break through the protective shield. It seems to me that the concept of trauma necessarily implies a connection of this kind with a breach in an otherwise efficacious barrier against stimuli. Such an event as an external trauma is bound to provoke a disturbance on a large scale in the functioning of the organism's energy and to set in motion every possible defensive measure. At the same time, the pleasure principle is for the moment put out of action. There is no longer any possibility of preventing the mental apparatus from being flooded with large amounts of stimulus, and another problem arises instead—the problem of mastering the amounts of stimulus which have broken in and of binding them, in the psychical

---

[11][Cf. 'Project', later part of Section 4 of Part I.]

sense, so that they can then be disposed of.

The specific unpleasure of physical pain is probably the result of the protective shield having been broken through in a limited area. There is then a continuous stream of excitations from the part of the periphery concerned to the central apparatus of the mind, such as could normally arise only from *within* the apparatus.[12] And how shall we expect the mind to react to this invasion? Cathectic energy is summoned from all sides to provide sufficiently high cathexes of energy in the environs of the breach. An 'anticathexis' on a grand scale is set up, for whose benefit all the other psychical systems are impoverished, so that the remaining psychical functions are extensively paralysed or reduced. We must endeavor to draw a lesson from examples such as this and use them as a basis for our metapsychological speculations. From the present case, then, we infer that a system which is itself highly cathected is capable of taking up an additional stream of fresh inflowing energy and of converting it into quiescent cathexis, that is of binding it psychically. The higher the system's own quiescent cathexis, the greater seems to be its binding force; conversely, therefore, the lower its cathexis, the less capacity will it have for taking up inflowing energy[13] and the more violent must be the consequences of such a breach in the protective shield against stimuli. To this view it cannot be justly objected that the increase of cathexis round the breach can be explained far more simply as the direct result of the inflowing masses of excitation. If that were so, the mental apparatus would merely receive an increase in its cathexes of energy, and the paralysing character of pain and the impoverishment of all

---

[12]Cf. 'Instincts and their Vicissitudes' (1915c) [and Addendum C of *Inhibitions, Symptoms and Anxiety* (1926d)].

[13][Cf. the 'principle of the insusceptibility to excitation of uncathected systems' in a footnote near the end of Freud, 1917d.]

the other systems would remain unexplained. Nor do the very violent phenomena of discharge to which pain gives rise affect our explanation, for they occur in a reflex manner— that is, they follow without the intervention of the mental apparatus. The indefiniteness of all our discussions on what we describe as metapsychology is of course due to the fact that we know nothing of the nature of the excitatory process that takes place in the elements of the psychical systems, and that we do not feel justified in framing any hypothesis on the subject. We are consequently operating all the time with a large unknown factor, which we are obliged to carry over into every new formula. It may be reasonably supposed that this excitatory process can be carried out with energies that vary *quantitatively;* it may also seem probable that it has more than one *quality* (in the nature of amplitude, for instance). As a new factor we have taken into consideration Breuer's hypothesis that charges of energy occur in two forms [see pp. 29–30]; so that we have to distinguish be- tween two kinds of cathexis of the psychical systems or their elements—a freely flowing cathexis that presses on towards discharge and a quiescent cathexis. We may perhaps suspect that the binding of the energy that streams into the mental apparatus consists in its change from a freely flowing into a quiescent state.

We may, I think, tentatively venture to regard the com- mon traumatic neurosis as a consequence of an extensive breach being made in the protective shield against stimuli. This would seem to reinstate the old, naive theory of shock, in apparent contrast to the later and psychologically more ambitious theory which attributes aetiological importance not to the effects of mechanical violence but to fright and the threat to life. These opposing views are not, however, irreconcilable; nor is the psycho-analytic view of the trau- matic neurosis identical with the shock theory in its crudest form. The latter regards the essence of the shock as being the direct damage to the molecular structure or even to the histological structure of the elements of the nervous system; whereas what *we* seek to understand are the effects produced on the organ of the mind by the breach in the shield against stimuli and by the problems that follow in its train. And we still attribute importance to the element of fright. It is caused by lack of any preparedness for anxiety,[14] including lack of hypercathexis of the systems that would be the first to receive the stimulus. Owing to their low cathexis those systems are not in a good position for binding the inflowing amounts of excitation and the consequences of the breach in the protective shield follow all the more easily. It will be seen, then, that preparedness for anxiety and the hypercathexis of the receptive systems constitute the last line of defence of the shield against stimuli. In the case of quite a number of traumas, the difference between systems that are unprepared and systems that are well prepared through being hypercathected may be a decisive factor in determining the outcome; though where the strength of a trauma exceeds a certain limit this factor will no doubt cease to carry weight. The fulfilment of wishes is, as we know, brought about in a hallucinatory manner by dreams, and under the dominance of the pleasure principle this has become their function. But it is not in the service of that principle that the dreams of patients suffering from traumatic neuroses lead them back with such regularity to the situation in which the trauma occurred. We may assume, rather, that dreams are here helping to carry out another task, which must be accomplished before the dominance of the pleasure principle can even begin. These dreams are

---

[14][Cf. footnote 3 on p. 11 above.]

endeavouring to master the stimulus retrospectively, by developing the anxiety whose omission was the cause of the traumatic neurosis. They thus afford us a view of a function of the mental apparatus which, though it does not contradict the pleasure principle, is nevertheless independent of it and seems to be more primitive than the purpose of gaining pleasure and avoiding unpleasure.

This would seem to be the place, then, at which to admit for the first time an exception to the proposition that dreams are fulfilments of wishes. Anxiety dreams, as I have shown repeatedly and in detail, offer no such exception. Nor do 'punishment dreams', for they merely replace the forbidden wish-fulfilment by the appropriate punishment for it; that is to say, they fulfil the wish of the sense of guilt which is the reaction to the repudiated impulse.[15] But it is impossible to classify as wish-fulfilments the dreams we have been discussing which occur in traumatic neuroses, or the dreams during psycho-analyses which bring to memory the psychical traumas of childhood. They arise, rather, in obedience to the compulsion to repeat, though it is true that in analysis that compulsion is supported by the wish (which is encouraged by 'suggestion')[16] to conjure up what has been forgotten and repressed. Thus it would seem that the function of dreams, which consists in setting aside any motives that might interrupt sleep, by fulfilling the wishes of the disturbing impulses, is not their *original* function. It would not be possible for them to perform that function until the whole of mental life had accepted the dominance of the pleasure principle. If

---

[15][See *The Interpretation of Dreams* (1900a), *Standard Ed.*, 5, 557, and Section 9 of Freud's 'Remarks on the Theory and Practice of Dream-Interpretation' (1923c).]
[16][The clause in brackets was substituted in 1923 for the words 'which is not unconscious' which appeared in the earlier editions.]

there is a 'beyond the pleasure principle', it is only consistent to grant that there was also a time before the purpose of dreams was the fulfilment of wishes. This would imply no denial of their later function. But if once this general rule has been broken, a further question arises. May not dreams which, with a view to the psychical binding of traumatic impressions, obey the compulsion to repeat—may not such dreams occur *outside* analysis as well? And the reply can only be a decided affirmative.

I have argued elsewhere[17] that 'war neuroses' (in so far as that term implies something more than a reference to the circumstances of the illness's onset) may very well be traumatic neuroses which have been facilitated by a conflict in the ego. The fact to which I have referred on pages 10–11, that a gross physical injury caused simultaneously by the trauma diminishes the chances that a neurosis will develop, becomes intelligible if one bears in mind two facts which have been stressed by psycho-analytic research: firstly, that mechanical agitation must be recognized as one of the sources of sexual excitation,[18] and secondly, that painful and feverish illnesses exercise a powerful effect, so long as they last, on the distribution of libido. Thus, on the one hand, the mechanical violence of the trauma would liberate a quantity of sexual excitation which, owing to the lack of preparation for anxiety, would have a traumatic effect; but, on the other hand, the simultaneous physical injury, by calling for a narcissistic hypercathexis of the injured organ,[19] would bind the excess of excitation. It is also well known, though the libido theory has not yet made sufficient use of the fact, that such severe disorders in the distribution of

---

[17]See my introduction (1919*d*) to *Psycho-Analysis and the War Neuroses.*
[18]Cf. my remarks elsewhere (*Three Essays* [*Standard Ed.*, 7, 201–2; *I.P.L.*, 57, 67–8]) on the effect of swinging and railway-travel.
[19]See my paper on narcissism (1914*c*) [Beginning of Section II].

libido as melancholia are temporarily brought to an end by intercurrent organic illness, and indeed that even a fully developed condition of dementia praecox is capable of a temporary remission in these same circumstances.

V

The fact that the cortical layer which receives stimuli is without any protective shield against excitations from within must have as its result that these latter transmissions of stimulus have a preponderance in economic importance and often occasion economic disturbances comparable with traumatic neuroses. The most abundant sources of this internal excitation are what are described as the organism's 'instincts'—the representatives of all the forces originating in the interior of the body and transmitted to the mental apparatus—at once the most important and the most obscure element of psychological research.

It will perhaps not be thought too rash to suppose that the impulses arising from the instincts do not belong to the type of *bound* nervous processes but of *freely mobile* processes which press towards discharge. The best part of what we know of these processes is derived from our study of the dream-work. We there discovered that the processes in the unconscious systems were fundamentally different from those in the preconscious (or conscious) systems. In the unconscious, cathexes can easily be completely transferred, displaced and condensed. Such treatment, however, could produce only invalid results if it were applied to preconscious material; and this accounts for the familiar peculiarities exhibited by manifest dreams after the preconscious residues of the preceding day have been worked over in accordance with the laws operating in the unconscious. I described the type of process found in the unconscious as the 'primary' psychical process, in contradistinction to the 'secondary' process which is the one obtaining in our normal waking life. Since all instinctual impulses have the unconscious systems as their point of impact, it is hardly an innovation to say that they obey the primary process. Again, it is easy to identify the primary psychical process with Breuer's freely mobile cathexis and the secondary process with changes in his bound or tonic cathexis.[1] If so, it would be the task of the higher strata of the mental apparatus to bind the instinctual excitation reaching the primary process. A failure to effect this binding would provoke a disturbance analogous to a traumatic neurosis; and only after the binding has been accomplished would it be possible for the dominance of the pleasure principle (and of its modification, the reality principle) to proceed unhindered. Till then the other task of the mental apparatus, the task of mastering or binding excitations, would have precedence—not, indeed, in *opposition* to the pleasure principle, but independently of it and to some extent in disregard of it.

The manifestations of a compulsion to repeat (which we have described as occurring in the early activities of infantile mental life as well as among the events of psycho-analytic treatment) exhibit to a high degree an instinctual[2] character and, when they act in opposition to the pleasure principle, give the appearance of some 'daemonic' force at work. In

---

[1] Cf. my *Interpretation of Dreams*, Chapter VII [*Standard Ed.*, 5, 588 ff. Cf. also Breuer and Freud, 1895 (Section 2 of Breuer's theoretical contribution)].

[2] [*'Triebhaft'* here and at the beginning of the next paragraph. The word *'Trieb'* bears much more of a feeling of urgency than the English 'instinct'.]

the case of children's play we seemed to see that children repeat unpleasurable experiences for the additional reason that they can master a powerful impression far more thoroughly by being active than they could by merely experiencing it passively. Each fresh repetition seems to strengthen the mastery they are in search of. Nor can children have their *pleasurable* experiences repeated often enough, and they are inexorable in their insistence that the repetition shall be an identical one. This character trait disappears later on. If a joke is heard for a second time it produces almost no effect; a theatrical production never creates so great an impression the second time as the first; indeed, it is hardly possible to persuade an adult who has very much enjoyed reading a book to re-read it immediately. Novelty is always the condition of enjoyment. But children will never tire of asking an adult to repeat a game that he has shown them or played with them, till he is too exhausted to go on. And if a child has been told a nice story, he will insist on hearing it over and over again rather than a new one; and he will remorselessly stipulate that the repetition shall be an identical one and will correct any alterations of which the narrator may be guilty—though they may actually have been made in the hope of gaining fresh approval.[3] None of this contradicts the pleasure principle; repetition, the re-experiencing of something identical, is clearly in itself a source of pleasure. In the case of a person in analysis, on the contrary, the compulsion to repeat the events of his childhood in the transference evidently disregards the pleasure principle in every way. The patient behaves in a purely infantile fashion and thus shows us that the repressed memory-traces of his primaeval experiences are not present in him in a bound

---

[3][Cf. some remarks on this towards the end of the sixth section of Chapter VII of Freud's book on jokes (1905*c*).]

state and are indeed in a sense incapable of obeying the secondary process. It is to this fact of not being bound, moreover, that they owe their capacity for forming, in conjunction with the residues of the previous day, a wishful phantasy that emerges in a dream. This same compulsion to repeat frequently meets us as an obstacle to our treatment when at the end of an analysis we try to induce the patient to detach himself completely from his physician. It may be presumed, too, that when people unfamiliar with analysis feel an obscure fear—a dread of rousing something that, so they feel, is better left sleeping—what they are afraid of at bottom is the emergence of this compulsion with its hint of possession by some 'daemonic' power.

But how is the predicate of being 'instinctual'[4] related to the compulsion to repeat? At this point we cannot escape a suspicion that we may have come upon the track of a universal attribute of instincts and perhaps of organic life in general which has not hitherto been clearly recognized or at least not explicitly stressed.[5] *It seems, then, that an instinct is an urge inherent in organic life to restore an earlier state of things* which the living entity has been obliged to abandon under the pressure of external disturbing forces; that is, it is a kind of organic elasticity, or, to put it another way, the expression of the inertia inherent in organic life.[6]

This view of instincts strikes us as strange because we have become used to see in them a factor impelling towards change and development, whereas we are now asked to recognize in them the precise contrary—an expression of the *conservative* nature of living substance. On the other hand we soon call to mind examples from animal life which

---

[4][See the last footnote but one.]
[5][The last six words were added in 1921.]
[6]I have no doubt that similar notions as to the nature of 'instincts' have already been put forward repeatedly.

seem to confirm the view that instincts are historically determined. Certain fishes, for instance, undertake laborious mi-
grations at spawning-time in order to deposit their spawn in
particular waters far removed from their customary haunts.
In the opinion of many biologists what they are doing is
merely to seek out the localities in which their species formerly resided but which in the course of time they have
exchanged for others. The same explanation is believed to
apply to the migratory flights of birds of passage—but we are
quickly relieved of the necessity for seeking for further examples by the reflection that the most impressive proofs of
there being an organic compulsion to repeat lie in the phenomena of heredity and the facts of embryology. We see
how the germ of a living animal is obliged in the course of
its development to recapitulate (even if only in a transient
and abbreviated fashion) the structures of all the forms from
which it is sprung, instead of proceeding quickly by the
shortest path to its final shape. This behaviour is only to a
very slight degree attributable to mechanical causes, and the
historical explanation cannot accordingly be neglected. So
too the power of regenerating a lost organ by growing afresh
a precisely similar one extends far up into the animal kingdom.

We shall be met by the plausible objection that it may
very well be that, in addition to the conservative instincts
which impel towards repetition, there may be others which
push forward towards progress and the production of new
forms. This argument must certainly not be overlooked, and
it will be taken into account at a later stage.[7] But for the
moment it is tempting to pursue to its logical conclusion the
hypothesis that all instincts tend towards the restoration of
an earlier state of things. The outcome may give an impres-

---

[7][The last half of this sentence was added in 1921.]

sion of mysticism or of sham profundity; but we can feel quite innocent of having had any such purpose in view. We seek only for the sober results of research or of reflection based on it; and we have no wish to find in those results any quality other than certainty.[8]

Let us suppose, then, that all the organic instincts are conservative, are acquired historically and tend towards the restoration of an earlier state of things. It follows that the phenomena of organic development must be attributed to external disturbing and diverting influences. The elementary living entity would from its very beginning have had no wish to change; if conditions remained the same, it would do no more than constantly repeat the same course of life. In the last resort, what has left its mark on the development of organisms must be the history of the earth we live in and of its relation to the sun. Every modification which is thus imposed upon the course of the organism's life is accepted by the conservative organic instincts and stored up for further repetition. Those instincts are therefore bound to give a deceptive appearance of being forces tending towards change and progress, whilst in fact they are merely seeking to reach an ancient goal by paths alike old and new. Moreover it is possible to specify this final goal of all organic striving. It would be in contradiction to the conservative nature of the instincts if the goal of life were a state of things which had never yet been attained. On the contrary, it must be an *old* state of things, an initial state from which the living entity has at one time or other departed and to which it is striving to return by the circuitous paths along which its development leads. If we are to take it as a truth that

---

[8][*Footnote added* 1925:] The reader should not overlook the fact that what follows is the development of an extreme line of thought. Later on, when account is taken of the sexual instincts, it will be found that the necessary limitations and corrections are applied to it.

knows no exception that everything living dies for *internal* reasons—becomes inorganic once again—then we shall be compelled to say that *'the aim of all life is death'* and, looking backwards, that *'inanimate things existed before living ones'.*

The attributes of life were at some time evoked in inanimate matter by the action of a force of whose nature we can form no conception. It may perhaps have been a process similar in type to that which later caused the development of consciousness in a particular stratum of living matter. The tension which then arose in what had hitherto been an inanimate substance endeavoured to cancel itself out. In this way the first instinct came into being: the instinct to return to the inanimate state. It was still an easy matter at that time for a living substance to die; the course of its life was probably only a brief one, whose direction was determined by the chemical structure of the young life. For a long time, perhaps, living substance was thus being constantly created afresh and easily dying, till decisive external influences altered in such a way as to oblige the still surviving substance to diverge ever more widely from its original course of life and to make ever more complicated *détours* before reaching its aim of death. These circuitous paths to death, faithfully kept to by the conservative instincts, would thus present us to-day with the picture of the phenomena of life. If we firmly maintain the exclusively conservative nature of instincts, we cannot arrive at any other notions as to the origin and aim of life.

The implications in regard to the great groups of instincts which, as we believe, lie behind the phenomena of life in organisms must appear no less bewildering. The hypothesis of self-preservative instincts, such as we attribute to all living beings, stands in marked opposition to the idea that instinctual life as a whole serves to bring about death. Seen in this light, the theoretical importance of the instincts of self-preservation, of self-assertion and of mastery greatly diminishes. They are component instincts whose function it is to assure that the organism shall follow its own path to death, and to ward off any possible ways of returning to inorganic existence other than those which are immanent in the organism itself. We have no longer to reckon with the organism's puzzling determination (so hard to fit into any context) to maintain its own existence in the face of every obstacle. What we are left with is the fact that the organism wishes to die only in its own fashion. Thus these guardians of life, too, were originally the myrmidons of death. Hence arises the paradoxical situation that the living organism struggles most energetically against events (dangers, in fact) which might help it to attain its life's aim rapidly—by a kind of short-circuit. Such behaviour is, however, precisely what characterizes purely instinctual as contrasted with intelligent efforts.[9]

But let us pause for a moment and reflect. It cannot be so. The sexual instincts, to which the theory of the neuroses gives a quite special place, appear under a very different aspect.

The external pressure which provokes a constantly increasing extent of development has not imposed itself upon *every* organism. Many have succeeded in remaining up to the present time at their lowly level. Many, though not all, such creatures, which must resemble the earliest stages of the higher animals and plants, are, indeed, living to-day. In the same way, the whole path of development to natural death is not trodden by *all* the elementary entities which compose the complicated body of one of the higher orga-

---

[9][In the editions before 1925 the following footnote appeared at this point. 'A correction of this extreme view of the self-preservative instincts follows.']

nisms. Some of them, the germ-cells, probably retain the original structure of living matter and, after a certain time, with their full complement of inherited and freshly acquired instinctual dispositions, separate themselves from the organism as a whole. These two characteristics may be precisely what enables them to have an independent existence. Under favourable conditions, they begin to develop—that is, to repeat the performance to which they owe their existence; and in the end once again one portion of their substance pursues its development to a finish, while another portion harks back once again as a fresh residual germ to the beginning of the process of development. These germ-cells, therefore, work against the death of the living substance and succeed in winning for it what we can only regard as potential immortality, though that may mean no more than a lengthening of the road to death. We must regard as in the highest degree significant the fact that this function of the germ-cell is reinforced, or only made possible, if it coalesces with another cell similar to itself and yet differing from it.

The instincts which watch over the destinies of these elementary organisms that survive the whole individual, which provide them with a safe shelter while they are defenceless against the stimuli of the external world, which bring about their meeting with other germ-cells, and so on—these constitute the group of the sexual instincts. They are conservative in the same sense as the other instincts in that they bring back earlier states of living substance; but they are conservative to a higher degree in that they are peculiarly resistant to external influences; and they are conservative too in another sense in that they preserve life itself for a comparatively long period.[10] They are the true life

---

[10][*Footnote added* 1923:] Yet it is to them alone that we can attribute an internal impulse towards 'progress' and towards higher development! (See

instincts. They operate against the purpose of the other instincts, which leads, by reason of their function, to death; and this fact indicates that there is an opposition between them and the other instincts, an opposition whose importance was long ago recognized by the theory of the neuroses. It is as though the life of the organism moved with a vacillating rhythm. One group of instincts rushes forward so as to reach the final aim of life as swiftly as possible; but when a particular stage in the advance has been reached, the other group jerks back to a certain point to make a fresh start and so prolong the journey. And even though it is certain that sexuality and the distinction between the sexes did not exist when life began, the possibility remains that the instincts which were later to be described as sexual may have been in operation from the very first, and it may not be true that it was only at a later time that they started upon their work of opposing the activities of the 'ego-instincts'.[11]

Let us now hark back for a moment ourselves and consider whether there is any basis at all for these speculations. Is it really the case that, *apart from the sexual instincts,*[12] there are no instincts that do not seek to restore an earlier state of things? that there are none that aim at a state of things which has never yet been attained? I know of no certain example from the organic world that would contradict the characterization I have thus proposed. There is unquestionably no universal instinct towards higher development observable in the animal or plant world, even though it is undeniable that development does in fact occur

[11][*Footnote added* 1925:] It should be understood from the context that the term 'ego-instincts' is used here as a provisional description and derives from the earliest psycho-analytical terminology. [See below, pp. 61 and 73–74.]
[12][These five words were italicized from 1921 onwards.]

in that direction. But on the one hand it is often merely a matter of opinion when we declare that one stage of development is higher than another, and on the other hand biology teaches us that higher development in one respect is very frequently balanced or outweighed by involution in another. Moreover there are plenty of animal forms from whose early stages we can infer that their development has, on the contrary, assumed a retrograde character. Both higher development and involution might well be the consequences of adaptation to the pressure of external forces; and in both cases the part played by instincts might be limited to the retention (in the form of an internal source of pleasure) of an obligatory modification.[13]

It may be difficult, too, for many of us, to abandon the belief that there is an instinct towards perfection at work in human beings, which has brought them to their present high level of intellectual achievement and ethical sublimation and which may be expected to watch over their development into supermen. I have no faith, however, in the existence of any such internal instinct and I cannot see how this benevolent illusion is to be preserved. The present development of human beings requires, as it seems to me, no different explanation from that of animals. What appears in a minority of human individuals as an untiring impulsion towards further perfection can easily be understood as a result of the instinctual repression upon which is based all that is most precious in human civilization. The repressed instinct never ceases to strive for complete satisfaction, which would consist in the repetition of a primary experi-

---

[13]Ferenczi (1913, 137) has reached the same conclusion along different lines: 'If this thought is pursued to its logical conclusion, one must make oneself familiar with the idea of a tendency to perseveration or regression dominating organic life as well, while the tendency to further development, to adaptation, etc., would become active only as a result of external stimuli.'

ence of satisfaction. No substitutive or reactive formations and no sublimations will suffice to remove the repressed instinct's persisting tension; and it is the difference in amount between the pleasure of satisfaction which is *demanded* and that which is actually *achieved* that provides the driving factor which will permit of no halting at any position attained, but, in the poet's words, '*ungebändigt immer vorwärts dringt*'.[14] The backward path that leads to complete satisfaction is as a rule obstructed by the resistances which maintain the repressions. So there is no alternative but to advance in the direction in which growth is still free—though with no prospect of bringing the process to a conclusion or of being able to reach the goal. The processes involved in the formation of a neurotic phobia, which is nothing else than an attempt at flight from the satisfaction of an instinct, present us with a model of the manner of origin of this supposititious 'instinct towards perfection'—an instinct which cannot possibly be attributed to *every* human being. The *dynamic* conditions for its development are, indeed, universally present; but it is only in rare cases that the *economic* situation appears to favour the production of the phenomenon.

I will add only a word to suggest that the efforts of Eros to combine organic substances into ever larger unities probably provide a substitute for this 'instinct towards perfection' whose existence we cannot admit. The phenomena that are attributed to it seem capable of explanation by these efforts of Eros taken in conjunction with the results of repression.[15]

---

[14]['Presses ever forward unsubdued.'] Mephistopheles in *Faust*, Part I [Scene 4].

[15][This paragraph, which was added in 1923, anticipates the account of Eros that is to follow in the next chapter, p. 60 ff.]

VI

The upshot of our enquiry so far has been the drawing of
a sharp distinction between the 'ego-instincts' and the sexual
instincts, and the view that the former exercise pressure
towards death and the latter towards a prolongation of life.
But this conclusion is bound to be unsatisfactory in many
respects even to ourselves. Moreover, it is actually only of
the former group of instincts that we can predicate a conservative, or rather retrograde, character corresponding to
a compulsion to repeat. For on our hypothesis the ego-
instincts arise from the coming to life of inanimate matter
and seek to restore the inanimate state; whereas as regards
the sexual instincts, though it is true that they reproduce
primitive states of the organism, what they are clearly aim-
ing at by every possible means is the coalescence of two
germ-cells which are differentiated in a particular way. If
this union is not effected, the germ-cell dies along with all
the other elements of the multicellular organism. It is only
on this condition that the sexual function can prolong the
cell's life and lend it the appearance of immortality. But
what is the important event in the development of living
substance which is being repeated in sexual reproduction, or
in its fore-runner, the conjugation of two protista?[1] We
cannot say; and we should consequently feel relieved if the

whole structure of our argument turned out to be mistaken. The opposition between the ego or death instincts[2] and the sexual or life instincts would then cease to hold and the compulsion to repeat would no longer possess the importance we have ascribed to it.

Let us turn back, then, to one of the assumptions that we have already made, with the exception that we shall be able to give it a categorical denial. We have drawn far-reaching conclusions from the hypothesis that all living substance is bound to die from internal causes. We made this assumption thus carelessly because it does not seem to us to *be* an assumption. We are accustomed to think that such is the fact, and we are strengthened in our thought by the writings of our poets. Perhaps we have adopted the belief because there is some comfort in it. If we are to die ourselves, and first to lose in death those who are dearest to us, it is easier to submit to a remorseless law of nature, to the sublime 'Aνάγχη [Necessity], than to a chance which might perhaps have been escaped. It may be, however, that this belief in the internal necessity of dying is only another of those illusions which we have created *'um die Schwere des Daseins zu ertragen'.*[3] It is certainly not a primaeval belief. The notion of 'natural death' is quite foreign to primitive races; they attribute every death that occurs among them to the influence of an enemy or of an evil spirit. We must therefore turn to biology in order to test the validity of the belief.

If we do so, we may be astonished to find how little agreement there is among biologists on the subject of natu-

---

[1][In what follows Freud appears to use the terms 'protista' and 'protozoa' indifferently to signify unicellular organisms. The translation follows the original.]
[2][The first published appearance of the term.]
[3]['To bear the burden of existence.' (Schiller, *Die Braut von Messina*, I, 8.]

ral death and in fact that the whole concept of death melts away under their hands. The fact that there is a fixed average duration of life at least among the higher animals naturally argues in favour of there being such a thing as death from natural causes. But this impression is countered when we consider that certain large animals and certain gigantic arboreal growths reach a very advanced age and one which cannot at present be computed. According to the large conception of Wilhelm Fliess [1906], all the phenomena of life exhibited by organism—and also, no doubt, their death— are linked with the completion of fixed periods, which express the dependence of two kinds of living substance (one male and the other female) upon the solar year. When we see, however, how easily and how extensively the influence of external forces is able to modify the date of the appearance of vital phenomena (especially in the plant world)—to precipitate them or hold them back—doubts must be cast upon the rigidity of Fliess's formulas or at least upon whether the laws laid down by him are the sole determining factors.

The greatest interest attaches from our point of view to the treatment given to the subject of the duration of life and the death of organisms in the writings of Weismann (1882, 1884, 1892, etc.) It was he who introduced the division of living substance into mortal and immortal parts. The mortal part is the body in the narrower sense—the 'soma'—which alone is subject to natural death. The germ-cells, on the other hand, are potentially immortal, in so far as they are able, under certain favourable conditions, to develop into a new individual, or, in other words, to surround themselves with a new soma. (Weismann, 1884.)

What strikes us in this is the unexpected analogy with our own view, which was arrived at along such a different path. Weismann, regarding living substance morphologically, sees in it one portion which is destined to die—the soma, the body apart from the substance concerned with sex and inheritance—and an immortal portion—the germ-plasm, which is concerned with the survival of the species, with reproduction. We, on the other hand, dealing not with the living substance but with the forces operating in it, have been led to distinguish two kinds of instincts: those which seek to lead what is living to death, and others, the sexual instincts, which are perpetually attempting and achieving a renewal of life. This sounds like a dynamic corollary to Weismann's morphological theory.

But the appearance of a significant correspondence is dissipated as soon as we discover Weismann's views on the problem of death. For he only relates the distinction between the mortal soma and the immortal germ-plasm to *multicellular* organisms; in unicellular organisms the individual and the reproductive cell are still one and the same (Weismann, 1882, 38). Thus he considers that unicellular organisms are potentially immortal, and that death only makes its appearance with the multicellular metazoa. It is true that this death of the higher organisms is a natural one, a death from internal causes; but it is not founded on any primal characteristic of living substance (Weismann, 1884, 84) and cannot be regarded as an absolute necessity with its basis in the very nature of life (Weismann, 1882, 33). Death is rather a matter of expediency, a manifestation of adaptation to the external conditions of life; for, when once the cells of the body have been divided into soma and germ-plasm, an unlimited duration of individual life would become a quite pointless luxury. When this differentiation had been made in the multicellular organisms, death became possible and expedient. Since then, the soma of the higher organisms has died at fixed periods for internal reasons, while the protista have remained immortal. It is not the case, on the other hand, that reproduction was only introduced at the same time as death. On the contrary, it is a primal characteristic of living matter, like growth (from which it originated), and life has been continuous from its first beginning upon earth. (Weismann, 1884, 84 f.)

It will be seen at once that to concede in this way that higher organisms have a natural death is of very little help to us. For if death is a *late* acquisition of organisms, then there can be no question of there having been death instincts from the very beginning of life on this earth. Multicellular organisms may die for internal reasons, owing to defective differentiation or to imperfections in their metabolism, but the matter is of no interest from the point of view of our problem. An account of the origin of death such as this is moreover far less at variance with our habitual modes of thought than the strange assumption of 'death instincts'.

The discussion which followed upon Weismann's suggestions led, so far as I can see, to no conclusive results in any direction.[4] Some writers returned to the views of Goette (1883), who regarded death as a direct result of reproduction. Hartmann (1906, 29) does not regard the appearance of a 'dead body'—a dead portion of the living substance—as the criterion of death, but defines death as 'the termination of individual development'. In this sense protozoa too are mortal; in their case death always coincides with reproduction, but is to some extent obscured by it, since the whole substance of the parent animal may be transmitted directly into the young offspring.

Soon afterwards research was directed to the experimental testing on unicellular organisms of the alleged immortality of living substance. An American biologist, Woodruff, experimenting with a ciliate infusorian, the 'slipper-animal-

---

[4]Cf. Hartmann (1906), Lipschütz (1914) and Doflein (1919).

cule', which reproduces by fission into two individuals, persisted until the 3029th generation (at which point he broke off the experiment), isolating one of the part-products on each occasion and placing it in fresh water. This remote descendent of the first slipper-animalcule was just as lively as its ancestor and showed no signs of ageing or degeneration. Thus, in so far as figures of this kind prove anything, the immortality of the protista seemed to be experimentally demonstrable.[5]

Other experimenters arrived at different results. Maupas, Calkins and others, in contrast to Woodruff, found that after a certain number of divisions those infusoria become weaker, diminish in size, suffer the loss of some part of their organization and eventually die, unless certain recuperative measures are applied to them. If this is so, protozoa would appear to die after a phase of senescence exactly like the higher animals—thus completely contradicting Weismann's assertion that death is a late acquisition of living organisms.

From the aggregate of these experiments two facts emerge which seem to offer us a firm footing.

First: If two of the animalculae, at the moment before they show signs of senescence, are able to coalesce with each other, that is to 'conjugate' (soon after which they once more separate), they are saved from growing old and become 'rejuvenated'. Conjugation is no doubt the fore-runner of the sexual reproduction of higher creatures; it is as yet unconnected with propagation and is limited to the mixing of the substances of the two individuals. (Weismann's 'amphimixis'.) The recuperative effects of conjugation can, however, be replaced by certain stimulating agents, by alterations in the composition of the fluid which provides their

---

[5]For this and what follows see Lipschütz (1914, 26 and 52 ff.).

nourishment, by raising their temperature or by shaking them. We are reminded of the celebrated experiment made by J. Loeb, in which, by means of certain chemical stimuli, he induced segmentation in sea-urchins' eggs—a process which can normally occur only after fertilization.

Secondly: It is probable nevertheless that infusoria die a natural death as a result of their own vital processes. For the contradiction between Woodruff's findings and the others is due to his having provided each generation with fresh nutrient fluid. If he omitted to do so, he observed the same signs of senescence as the other experimenters. He concluded that the animalculae were injured by the products of metabolism which they extruded into the surrounding fluid. He was then able to prove conclusively that it was only the products of its *own* metabolism which had fatal results for the particular kind of animalcule. For the same animalculae which inevitably perished if they were crowded together in their own nutrient fluid flourished in a solution which was over-saturated with the waste products of a distantly related species. An infusorian, therefore, if it is left to itself, dies a natural death owing to its incomplete voidance of the products of its own metabolism. (It may be that the same incapacity is the ultimate cause of the death of all higher animals as well.)

At this point the question may well arise in our minds whether any object whatever is served by trying to solve the problem of natural death from a study of the protozoa. The primitive organization of these creatures may conceal from our eyes important conditions which, though in fact present in them too, only become *visible* in higher animals where they are able to find morphological expression. And if we abandon the morphological point of view and adopt the dynamic one, it becomes a matter of complete indifference to us whether natural death can be shown to occur in proto-

zoa or not. The substance which is later recognized as being
immortal has not yet become separated in them from the
mortal one. The instinctual forces which seek to conduct life
into death may also be operating in protozoa from the first,
and yet their effects may be so completely concealed by the
life-preserving forces that it may be very hard to find any
direct evidence of their presence. We have seen, moreover,
that the observations made by biologists allow us to assume
that internal processes of this kind leading to death do occur
also in protista. But even if protista turned out to be immortal in Weismann's sense, his assertion that death is a late
acquisition would apply only to its *manifest* phenomena and
would not make impossible the assumption of processes
tending towards it.

Thus our expectation that biology would flatly contradict
the recognition of death instincts has not been fulfilled. We
are at liberty to continue concerning ourselves with their
possibility, if we have other reasons for doing so. The striking similarity between Weismann's distinction of soma and
germ-plasm and our separation of the death instincts from
the life instincts persists and retains its significance.

We may pause for a moment over this pre-eminently
dualistic view of instinctual life. According to E. Hering's
theory, two kinds of processes are constantly at work in
living substance, operating in contrary directions, one constructive or assimilatory and the other destructive or dis-
similatory. May we venture to recognize in these two directions taken by the vital processes the activity of our two
instinctual impulses, the life instincts and the death instincts? There is something else, at any rate, that we cannot
remain blind to. We have unwittingly steered our course
into the harbour of Schopenhauer's philosophy. For him
death is the 'true result and to that extent the purpose of
life',[6] while the sexual instinct is the embodiment of the will

to live. (Cf. the Appendix to Freud, 1925*e*.]

Let us make a bold attempt at another step forward. It is generally considered that the union of a number of cells into a vital association—the multicellular character of organisms—has become a means of prolonging their life. One cell helps to preserve the life of another, and the community of cells can survive even if individual cells have to die. We have already heard that conjugation, too, the temporary coalescence of two unicellular organisms, has a life-preserving and rejuvenating effect on both of them. Accordingly, we might attempt to apply the libido theory which has been arrived at in psycho-analysis to the mutual relationship of cells. We might suppose that the life instincts or sexual instincts which are active in each cell take the other cells as their object, that they partly neutralize the death instincts (that is, the processes set up by them) in those cells and thus preserve their life; while the other cells do the same for *them,* and still others sacrifice themselves in the performance of this libidinal function. The germ-cells themselves would behave in a completely 'narcissistic' fashion—to use the phrase that we are accustomed to use in the theory of the neuroses to describe a whole individual who retains his libido in his ego and pays none of it out in object-cathexes. The germ-cells require their libido, the activity of their life instincts, for themselves, as a reserve against their later momentous constructive activity. (The cells of the malignant neoplasms which destroy the organism should also perhaps be described as narcissistic in this same sense: pathology is prepared to regard their germs as innate and to ascribe embryonic attributes to them.)[7] In this way the libido of our sexual instincts would coincide with the Eros of the poets

[6]Schopenhauer (1851; *Sämtliche Werke,* ed. Hübscher, 1938, 5, 236).
[7][This sentence was added in 1921.]

and philosophers which holds all living things together.

Here then is an opportunity for looking back over the slow development of our libido theory. In the first instance the analysis of the transference neuroses forced upon our notice the opposition between the 'sexual instincts', which are directed towards an object, and certain other instincts, with which we were very insufficiently acquainted and which we described provisionally as the 'ego-instincts'.[8] A foremost place among these was necessarily given to the instincts serving the self-preservation of the individual. It was impossible to say what other distinctions were to be drawn among them. No knowledge would have been more valuable as a foundation for true psychological science than an approximate grasp of the common characteristics and possible distinctive features of the instincts. But in no region of psychology were we groping more in the dark. Everyone assumed the existence of as many instincts or 'basic instincts' as he chose, and juggled with them like the ancient Greek natural philosophers with their four elements—earth, air, fire and water. Psycho-analysis, which could not escape making *some* assumption about the instincts, kept at first to the popular division of instincts typified in the phrase 'hunger and love'. At least there was nothing arbitrary in this; and by its help the analysis of the psychoneuroses was carried forward quite a distance. The concept of 'sexuality', and at the same time of the sexual instinct, had, it is true, to be extended so as to cover many things which could not be classed under the reproductive function; and this caused no little hubbub in an austere, respectable or merely hypocritical world.

The next step was taken when psycho-analysis felt its way closer towards the psychological ego, which it had first come

---

[8][So, for instance, in the account of this opposition given in Freud's paper on psychogenic disturbances of vision (1910*i*).]

to know only as a repressive, censoring agency, capable of erecting protective structures and reactive formations. Critical and farseeing minds had, it is true, long since objected to the concept of libido being restricted to the energy of the sexual instincts directed towards an object. But they failed to explain how they had arrived at their better knowledge or to derive from it anything of which analysis could make use. Advancing more cautiously, psycho-analysis observed the regularity with which libido is withdrawn from the object and directed on to the ego (the process of introversion); and, by studying the libidinal development of children in its earliest phases, came to the conclusion that the ego is the true and original reservoir of libido,[9] and that it is only from that reservoir that libido is extended on to objects. The ego now found its position among sexual objects and was at once given the foremost place among them. Libido which was in this way lodged in the ego was described as 'narcissistic'.[10] This narcissistic libido was of course also a manifestation of the force of the sexual instinct in the analytical sense of those words, and it had necessarily to be identified with the 'self-preservative instincts' whose existence had been recognized from the first. Thus the original opposition between the ego-instincts and the sexual instincts proved to be inadequate. A portion of the ego-instincts was seen to be libidinal; sexual instincts—probably alongside others—operated in the ego. Nevertheless we are justified in saying that the old formula which lays it down that psychoneuroses are based on a conflict between ego-instincts and sexual instincts contains nothing that we need reject to-day. It is merely that

---

[9][This idea was fully stated by Freud in his paper on narcissism (1914c), Section I. See, however, his later footnote, near the beginning of Chapter III of The Ego and the Id (1923b), in which he corrects this statement and describes the id as 'the great reservoir of libido'.]

[10]See my paper on narcissism (1914c) [Section I].

the distinction between the two kinds of instinct, which was originally regarded as in some sort of way *qualitative*, must now be characterized differently—namely as being *topo-graphical.* And in particular it is still true that the transference neuroses, the essential subject of psycho-analytic study, are the result of a conflict between the ego and the libidinal cathexis of objects.

But it is all the more necessary for us to lay stress upon the libidinal character of the self-preservative instincts now that we are venturing upon the further step of recognizing the sexual instinct as Eros, the preserver of all things, and of deriving the narcissistic libido of the ego from the stores of libido by means of which the cells of the soma are attached to one another. But we now find ourselves suddenly faced by another question. If the self-preservative instincts too are of a libidinal nature, are there perhaps no other instincts whatever but the libidinal ones? At all events there are none other visible. But in that case we shall after all be driven to agree with the critics who suspected from the first that psycho-analysis explains *everything* by sexuality, or with innovators like Jung who, making a hasty judgement, have used the word 'libido' to mean instinctual force in general. Must not this be so?

It was not our *intention* at all events to produce such a result. Our argument had as its point of departure a sharp distinction between ego-instincts, which we equated with death instincts, and sexual instincts, which we equated with life instincts. (We were prepared at one stage [p. 46] to include the so-called self-preservative instincts of the ego among the death instincts; but we subsequently [p. 62] corrected ourselves on this point and withdrew it.) Our views have from the very first been *dualistic*, and to-day they are even more definitely dualistic than before—now that we describe the opposition as being, not between ego-instincts and sexual instincts but between life instincts and death instincts. Jung's libido theory is on the contrary *monistic;* the fact that he has called his one instinctual force 'libido' is bound to create confusion, but need not affect us otherwise.[11] We suspect that instincts other than those of self-preservation operate in the ego, and it ought to be possible for us to point to them. Unfortunately, however, the analysis of the ego has made so little headway that it is very difficult for us to do so. It is possible, indeed, that the libidinal instincts in the ego may be linked in a peculiar manner[12] with these other ego-instincts which are still strange to us. Even before we had any clear understanding of narcissism, psycho-analysts had a suspicion that the 'ego-instincts' had libidinal components attached to them. But these are very uncertain possibilities, to which our opponents will pay very little attention. The difficulty remains that psycho-analysis has not enabled us hitherto to point to any [ego-] instincts other than the libidinal ones. That, however, is no reason for our falling in with the conclusion that no others in fact exist.

In the obscurity that reigns at present in the theory of the instincts, it would be unwise to reject any idea that promises to throw light on it. We started out from the great opposition between the life and death instincts. Now object-love itself presents us with a second example of a similar polarity—that between love (or affection) and hate (or aggressiveness). If only we could succeed in relating these two polarities to each other and in deriving one from the other! From the very first we recognized the presence of a sadistic component in the sexual instinct.[13] As we know, it can make itself

---

[11][The two preceding sentences were added in 1921.]
[12][In the first edition only: '—by instinctual "confluence", to borrow a term used by Adler [1908]—'.]
[13]This was already so in the first edition of *Three Essays on the Theory of Sexuality* in 1905 [*Standard Ed.*, 7, 157 ff.; *I.P.L.*, 57, 23 ff.].

independent and can, in the form of a perversion, dominate an individual's entire sexual activity. It also emerges as a predominant component instinct in one of the 'pregenital organizations', as I have named them. But how can the sadistic instinct, whose aim it is to injure the object, be derived from Eros, the preserver of life? Is it not plausible to suppose that this sadism is in fact a death instinct which, under the influence of the narcissistic libido, has been forced away from the ego and has consequently only emerged in relation to the object? It now enters the service of the sexual function. During the oral stage of organization of the libido, the act of obtaining erotic mastery over an object coincides with that object's destruction; later, the sadistic instinct separates off, and finally, at the stage of genital primacy, it takes on, for the purposes of reproduction, the function of overpowering the sexual object to the extent necessary for carrying out the sexual act. It might indeed be said that the sadism which has been forced out of the ego has pointed the way for the libidinal components of the sexual instinct, and that these follow after it to the object. Wherever the original sadism has undergone no mitigation or intermixture, we find the familiar ambivalence of love and hate in erotic life.[14]

If such an assumption as this is permissible, then we have met the demand that we should produce an example of a death instinct—though, it is true, a displaced one. But this way of looking at things is very far from being easy to grasp and creates a positively mystical impression. It looks suspiciously as though we were trying to find a way out of a highly embarrassing situation at any price. We may recall, however, that there is nothing new in an assumption of this kind. We put one forward on an earlier occasion, before there was

---

[14][This foreshadows Freud's discussion of instinctual 'fusion' in Chap. IV of *The Ego and the Id* (1923*b*).]

any question of an embarrassing situation. Clinical observations led us at that time to the view that masochism, the component instinct which is complementary to sadism, must be regarded as sadism that has been turned round upon the subject's own ego.[15] But there is no difference in principle between an instinct turning from an object to the ego and its turning from the ego to an object—which is the new point now under discussion. Masochism, the turning round of the instinct upon the subject's own ego, would in that case be a return to an earlier phase of the instinct's history, a regression. The account that was formerly given of masochism requires emendation as being too sweeping in one respect: there *might* be such a thing as primary masochism—a possibility which I had contested at that time.[16]

Let us, however, return to the self-preservative sexual instincts. The experiments upon protista have already shown us that conjugation—that is, the coalescence of two individuals which separate soon afterwards without any subsequent cell-division occurring—has a strengthening and rejuvenating effect upon both of them.[17] In later generations they show no signs of degenerating and seem able to put up a longer resistance to the injurious effects of their

---

[15]See my *Three Essays* (1905d) [*Standard Ed.*, 7, 158; *I.P.L.*, 57, 24]; and 'Instincts and their Vicissitudes' (1915c).

[16]A considerable portion of these speculations have been anticipated by Sabina Spielrein (1912) in an instructive and interesting paper which, however, is unfortunately not entirely clear to me. She there describes the sadistic components of the sexual instinct as 'destructive'. A. Stärke (1914), again, has attempted to identify the concept of libido itself with the biological concept (assumed on theoretical grounds) of an impetus towards death. See also Rank (1907). All these discussions, like that in the text, give evidence of the demand for a clarification of the theory of the instincts such as has not yet been achieved.—[A later discussion of the destructive instinct by Freud himself occupies Chapter VI of *Civilization and its Discontents* (1930a).]

[17]See the account quoted above, pp. 57–58, from Lipschütz (1914).

own metabolism. This single observation may, I think, be taken as typical of the effect produced by sexual union as well. But how is it that the coalescence of two only slightly different cells can bring about this renewal of life? The experiment which replaces the conjugation of protozoa by the application of chemical or even of mechanical stimuli (cf. Lipschütz, 1914) enables us to give what is no doubt a conclusive reply to this question. The result is brought about by the influx of fresh amounts of stimulus. This tallies well with the hypothesis that the life process of the individual leads for internal reasons to an abolition of chemical tensions, that is to say, to death, whereas union with the living substance of a different individual increases those tensions, introducing what may be described as fresh 'vital differences' which must then be lived off. As regards this dissimilarity there must of course be one or more optima. The dominating tendency of mental life, and perhaps of nervous life in general, is the effort to reduce, to keep constant or to remove internal tension due to stimuli (the 'Nirvana principle', to borrow a term from Barbara Low [1920, 73])—a tendency which finds expression in the pleasure principle;[18] and our recognition of that fact is one of our strongest reasons for believing in the existence of death instincts.

But we still feel our line of thought appreciably hampered by the fact that we cannot ascribe to the sexual instinct the characteristic of a compulsion to repeat which first put us on the track of the death instincts. The sphere of embryonic developmental processes is no doubt extremely rich in such phenomena of repetition; the two germ-cells that are involved in sexual reproduction and their life history are them-

---

[18][Cf. p. 1 ff. The whole topic is further considered in 'The Economic Problem of Masochism' (1924c).]

selves only repetitions of the beginnings of organic life. But
the essence of the processes to which sexual life is directed
is the coalescence of two cell-bodies. That alone is what
guarantees the immortality of the living substance in the
higher organisms.

In other words, we need more information on the origin
of sexual reproduction and of the sexual instincts in general.
This is a problem which is calculated to daunt an outsider
and which the specialists themselves have not yet been able
to solve. We shall therefore give only the briefest summary
of whatever seems relevant to our line of thought from
among the many discordant assertions and opinions.

One of these views deprives the problem of reproduction
of its mysterious fascination by representing it as a part
manifestation of growth. (Cf. multiplication by fission,
sprouting or gemmation.) The origin of reproduction by
sexually differentiated germ-cells might be pictured along
sober Darwinian lines by supposing that the advantage of
amphimixis, arrived at on some occasion by the chance
conjugation of two protista, was retained and further exploited in later development.[19] On this view 'sex' would not
be anything very ancient; and the extraordinarily violent
instincts whose aim it is to bring about sexual union would
be repeating something that had once occurred by chance
and had since become established as being advantageous.

The question arises here, as in the case of death [p. 58],
whether we do right in ascribing to protista those character-

---

[19]Though Weismann (1892) denies this advantage as well: 'In no case does
fertilization correspond to a rejuvenescence or renewal of life, nor is its
occurrence necessary in order that life may endure: it is merely an arrange-
ment which renders possible the intermingling of two different hereditary
tendencies.' [English translation, 1893, 231.] He nevertheless believes that
an intermingling of this kind leads to an increase in the variability of the
organism concerned.

istics alone which they actually exhibit, and whether it is correct to assume that forces and processes which become visible only in the higher organisms originated in those organisms for the first time. The view of sexuality we have just mentioned is of little help for our purposes. The objection may be raised against it that it postulates the existence of life instincts already operating in the simplest organisms; for otherwise conjugation, which works counter to the course of life and makes the task of ceasing to live more difficult, would not be retained and elaborated but would be avoided. If, therefore, we are not to abandon the hypothesis of death instincts, we must suppose them to be associated from the very first with life instincts. But it must be admitted that in that case we shall be working upon an equation with two unknown quantities.

Apart from this, science has so little to tell us about the origin of sexuality that we can liken the problem to a darkness into which not so much as a ray of a hypothesis has penetrated. In quite a different region, it is true, we *do* meet with such a hypothesis; but it is of so fantastic a kind—a myth rather than a scientific explanation—that I should not venture to produce it here, were it not that it fulfils precisely the one condition whose fulfilment we desire. For it traces the origin of an instinct to *a need to restore an earlier state of things.*

What I have in mind is, of course, the theory which Plato put into the mouth of Aristophanes in the *Symposium,* and which deals not only with the *origin* of the sexual instinct but also with the most important of its variations in relation to its object. 'The original human nature was not like the present, but different. In the first place, the sexes were originally three in number, not two as they are now; there was man, woman, and the union of the two. . . .' Everything about these primaeval men was double: they had four hands and four feet, two faces, two privy parts, and so on. Eventually Zeus decided to cut these men in two, 'like a sorb-apple which is halved for pickling'. After the division had been made, 'the two parts of man, each desiring his other half, came together, and threw their arms about one another eager to grow into one'.[20]

Shall we follow the hint given us by the poet-philosopher, and venture upon the hypothesis that living substance at the time of its coming to life was torn apart into small particles, which have ever since endeavoured to reunite through the sexual instincts? that these instincts, in which the chemical affinity of inanimate matter persisted, gradually succeeded,

---

[20][Jowett's translation. *Footnote added* 1921:] I have to thank Professor Heinrich Gomperz, of Vienna, for the following discussion on the origin of the Platonic myth, which I give partly in his own words. It is to be remarked that what is essentially the same theory is already to be found in the Upanishads. For we find the following passage in the *Brihadâranyaka-upanishad*, 1, 4, 3 [Max-Müller's translation, 2, 85 f.], where the origin of the world from the Atman (the Self or Ego) is described: 'But he felt no delight. Therefore a man who is lonely feels no delight. He wished for a second. He was so large as man and wife together. He then made this his Self to fall in two, and then arose husband and wife. Therefore Yagñavalkya said: "We two are thus (each of us) like half a shell." Therefore the void which was there, is filled by the wife.'

The *Brihadâranyaka-upanishad* is the most ancient of all the Upanishads, and no competent authority dates it later than about the year 800 B.C. In contradiction to the prevailing opinion, I should hesitate to give an unqualified denial to the possibility of Plato's myth being derived, even if it were only indirectly, from the Indian source, since a similar possibility cannot be excluded in the case of the doctrine of transmigration. But even if a derivation of this kind (through the Pythagoreans in the first instance) were established, the significance of the coincidence between the two trains of thought would scarcely be diminished. For Plato would not have adopted a story of this kind which had somehow reached him through some oriental tradition—to say nothing of giving it so important a place—unless it had struck him as containing an element of truth.

In a paper devoted to a systematic examination of this line of thought before the time of Plato, Ziegler (1913) traces it back to Babylonian origins.

[Freud had already alluded to Plato's myth in his *Three Essays, Standard Ed.*, 7, 136; *I.P.L.*, 57, 2.]

as they developed through the kingdom of the protista, in overcoming the difficulties put in the way of that endeavour by an environment charged with dangerous stimuli—stimuli which compelled them to form a protective cortical layer? that these splintered fragments of living substance in this way attained a multicellular condition and finally transferred the instinct for reuniting, in the most highly concentrated form, to the germ-cells?—But here, I think, the moment has come for breaking off.

Not, however, without the addition of a few words of critical reflection. It may be asked whether and how far I am myself convinced of the truth of the hypotheses that have been set out in these pages. My answer would be that I am not convinced myself and that I do not seek to persuade other people to believe in them. Or, more precisely, that I do not know how far I believe in them. There is no reason, as it seems to me, why the emotional factor of conviction should enter into this question at all. It is surely possible to throw oneself into a line of thought and to follow it wherever it leads out of simple scientific curiosity, or, if the reader prefers, as an *advocatus diaboli*, who is not on that account himself sold to the devil. I do not dispute the fact that the third step in the theory of the instincts, which I have taken here, cannot lay claim to the same degree of certainty as the two earlier ones—the extension of the concept of sexuality and the hypothesis of narcissism. These two innovations were a direct translation of observation into theory and were no more open to sources of error than is inevitable in all such cases. It is true that my assertion of the regressive character of instincts also rests upon observed material—namely on the facts of the compulsion to repeat. It may be, however, that I have overestimated their significance. And in any case it is impossible to pursue an idea of this kind except by repeatedly combining factual material with what is purely

speculative and thus diverging widely from empirical observation. The more frequently this is done in the course of
constructing a theory, the more untrustworthy, as we know,
must be the final result. But the degree of uncertainty is not
assignable. One may have made a lucky hit or one may have
gone shamefully astray. I do not think a large part is played
by what is called 'intuition' in work of this kind. From what
I have seen of intuition, it seems to me to be the product
of a kind of intellectual impartiality. Unfortunately, however, people are seldom impartial where ultimate things, the
great problems of science and life, are concerned. Each of
us is governed in such cases by deep-rooted internal prejudices, into whose hands our speculation unwittingly plays.
Since we have such good grounds for being distrustful, our
attitude towards the results of our own deliberations cannot
well be other than one of cool benevolence. I hasten to add,
however, that self-criticism such as this is far from binding
one to any special tolerance towards dissentient opinions. It
is perfectly legitimate to reject remorselessly theories which
are contradicted by the very first steps in the analysis of
observed facts, while yet being aware at the same time that
the validity of one's own theory is only a provisional one.

We need not feel greatly disturbed in judging our speculation upon the life and death instincts by the fact that so
many bewildering and obscure processes occur in it—such
as one instinct being driven out by another or an instinct
turning from the ego to an object, and so on. This is merely
due to our being obliged to operate with the scientific terms,
that is to say with the figurative language, peculiar to psychology (or, more precisely, to depth psychology). We could
not otherwise describe the processes in question at all, and
indeed we could not have become aware of them. The
deficiencies in our description would probably vanish if we
were already in a position to replace the psychological terms

by physiological or chemical ones. It is true that they too are only part of a figurative language; but it is one with which we have long been familiar and which is perhaps a simpler one as well.

On the other hand it should be made quite clear that the uncertainty of our speculation has been greatly increased by the necessity for borrowing from the science of biology. Biology is truly a land of unlimited possibilities. We may expect it to give us the most surprising information and we cannot guess what answers it will return in a few dozen years to the questions we have put to it. They may be of a kind which will blow away the whole of our artificial structure of hypotheses. If so, it may be asked why I have embarked upon such a line of thought as the present one, and in particular why I have decided to make it public. Well—I cannot deny that some of the analogies, correlations and connections which it contains seemed to me to deserve consideration.[21]

---

[21] I will add a few words to clarify our terminology, which has undergone some development in the course of the present work. We came to know what the 'sexual instincts' were from their relation to the sexes and to the reproductive function. We retained this name after we had been obliged by the findings of psycho-analysis to connect them less closely with reproduction. With the hypothesis of narcissistic libido and the extension of the concept of libido to the individual cells, the sexual instinct was transformed for us into Eros, which seeks to force together and hold together the portions of living substance. What are commonly called the sexual instincts are looked upon by us as the part of Eros which is directed towards objects. Our speculations have suggested that Eros operates from the beginning of life and appears as a 'life instinct' in opposition to the 'death instinct' which was brought into being by the coming to life of inorganic substance. These speculations seek to solve the riddle of life by supposing that these two instincts were struggling with each other from the very first. [*Added* 1921:] It is not so easy, perhaps, to follow the transformations through which the concept of the 'ego-instincts' has passed. To begin with we applied that name to all the instinctual trends (of which we had no closer knowledge) which could be distinguished from the sexual instincts directed towards an object; and we opposed the ego-instincts to the sexual instincts of which

VII

If it is really the case that seeking to restore an earlier state of things is such a universal characteristic of instincts, we need not be surprised that so many processes take place in mental life independently of the pleasure principle. This characteristic would be shared by all the component instincts and in their case would aim at returning once more to a particular stage in the course of development. These are matters over which the pleasure principle has as yet no control; but it does not follow that any of them are necessarily opposed to it, and we have still to solve the problem of the relation of the instinctual processes of repetition to the dominance of the pleasure principle.

We have found that one of the earliest and most important functions of the mental apparatus is to bind the instinctual impulses which impinge on it, to replace the primary process prevailing in them by the secondary process and convert their freely mobile cathectic energy into a mainly quiescent (tonic) cathexis. While this transformation is taking place no attention can be paid to the development of unpleasure; but this does not imply the suspension of the pleasure principle. On the contrary, the transformation occurs on *behalf* of the pleasure principle; the binding is a preparatory act which introduces and assures the dominance of the pleasure principle.

Let us make a sharper distinction than we have hitherto made between function and tendency. The pleasure principle, then, is a tendency operating in the service of a function whose business it is to free the mental apparatus entirely from excitation or to keep the amount of excitation in it constant or to keep it as low as possible. We cannot yet decide with certainty in favour of any of these ways of putting it; but it is clear that the function thus described would be concerned with the most universal endeavour of all living substance—namely to return to the quiescence of the inorganic world. We have all experienced how the greatest pleasure attainable by us, that of the sexual act, is associated with a momentary extinction of a highly intensified excitation. The binding of an instinctual impulse would be a preliminary function designed to prepare the excitation for its final elimination in the pleasure of discharge.

This raises the question of whether feelings of pleasure and unpleasure can be produced equally from bound and from unbound excitatory processes. And there seems to be no doubt whatever that the unbound or primary processes give rise to far more intense feelings in both directions than the bound or secondary ones. Moreover the primary processes are the earlier in time; at the beginning of mental life there are no others, and we may infer that if the pleasure principle had not already been operative in *them* it could never have been established for the later ones. We thus reach what is at bottom no very simple conclusion, namely that at the beginning of mental life the struggle for pleasure was far more intense than later but not so unrestricted: it had to submit to frequent interruptions. In later times the dominance of the pleasure principle is very much more secure, but it itself has no more escaped the process of taming than the other instincts in general. In any case, whatever it is that causes the appearance of feelings of pleasure and unpleasure in processes of excitation must be present in the secondary process just as it is in the primary one.

Here might be the starting-point for fresh investigations. Our consciousness communicates to us feelings from within not only of pleasure and unpleasure but also of a peculiar tension which in its turn can be either pleasurable or unpleasurable. Should the difference between these feelings enable us to distinguish between bound and unbound processes of energy? or is the feeling of tension to be related to the absolute magnitude, or perhaps to the level, of the cathexis, while the pleasure and unpleasure series indicates a change in the magnitude of the cathexis *within a given unit of time?*[1] Another striking fact is that the life instincts have so much more contact with our internal perception—emerging as breakers of the peace and constantly producing tensions whose release is felt as pleasure—while the death instincts seem to do their work unobtrusively. The pleasure principle seems actually to serve the death instincts. It is true that it keeps watch upon stimuli from without, which are regarded as dangers by both kinds of instincts; but it is more especially on guard against increases of stimulation from within, which would make the task of living more difficult. This in turn raises a host of other questions to which we can at present find no answer. We must be patient and await fresh methods and occasions of research. We must be ready, too, to abandon a path that we have followed for a time, if it seems to be leading to no good end. Only believers, who demand that science shall be a substitute for

---

[1][Cf. above, p. 4. These questions had already been touched on by Freud in his 'Project', e.g. in Part I, Section 8 and Part III, Section 1.]

the catechism they have given up, will blame an investigator
for developing or even transforming his views. We may take
comfort, too, for the slow advances of our scientific knowledge in the words of the poet:

Was man nicht erfliegen kann, muss man erhinken.

Die Schrift sagt, es ist keine Sünde zu hinken. [2]

[2] ['What we cannot reach flying we must reach limping. . . . The Book tells
us it is no sin to limp.' The last lines of 'Die beiden Gulden', a version by
Rückert of one of the *Maqâmât* of al-Hariri. Freud also quoted these lines
in a letter to Fliess of Oct. 20, 1895 (Freud 1950*a*, Letter 32).]

LIST OF ABBREVIATIONS

G.S.	= Freud, *Gesammelte Schriften* (12 vols.), Vienna, 1924–34.
G.W.	= Freud, *Gesammelte Werke* (18 vols), London, from 1940.
C.P.	= Freud, *Collected Papers* (5 vols.), London, 1924–50.
S.E. *Standard Ed.* }	= Freud, *Standard Edition* (24 vols.), London, from 1953.
I.P.L.	= *International Psycho-Analytical Library*, Hogarth Press and Institute of Psycho-Analysis, London, from 1921.
Theoretische Schriften	= Freud, *Theoretische Schriften (1911–25)*, Vienna, 1931.

BIBLIOGRAPHY
AND AUTHOR INDEX

[TITLES of books and periodicals are in italics; titles of papers are in inverted commas. Abbreviations are in accordance with the *World List of Scientific Periodicals* (London, 1952). Further abbreviations used in this volume will be found in the List on page 79. Numerals in thick type refer to volumes; ordinary numerals refer to pages. The figures in round brackets at the end of each entry indicate the page or pages of this volume on which the work in question is mentioned. In the case of the Freud entries, the letters attached to the dates of publication are in accordance with the corresponding entries in the complete bibliography of Freud's writings to be included in the last volume of the *Standard Edition*.

For non-technical authors, and for technical authors where no specific work is mentioned, see the General Index.]

ADLER, A. (1908) 'Der Aggressionsbetrieb im Leben und in der Neurose',
    Fortschr. Med., No. 19. (64)
BREUER, J., and FREUD, S. (1893) See FREUD, S. (1893*a*)
    (1895) See FREUD, S. (1895*d*)
    (1940) See FREUD, S. (1940*d*)
DOFLEIN, F. (1919) *Das Problem des Todes und der Unsterblichkeit bei*
    den Pflanzen und Tieren, Jena. (56)
FECHNER, G. T. (1873) *Einige Ideen zur Schöpfungs- und Entwick-*
    lungsgeschichte der Organismen, Leipzig. (5, 6)
FERENCZI, S. (1913) 'Entwicklungsstufen des Wirklichkeitssinnes', *Int.*
    Z. Psychoanal., **1**, 124. (50)
    [*Trans.:* 'Stages in the Development of the Sense of Reality', *First*
    Contributions to Psycho-Analysis, London, 1952, Chap. VIII.]
FLIESS, W. (1906) *Der Ablauf des Lebens*, Vienna. (54)
FREUD, S. (1893*a*) With BREUER, J., 'Über den psychischen Me-

chanismus hysterischer Phänomene: Vorläufige Mitteilung', *G.S.*, 1, 7; *G.W.*, 1, 81. (12)
[*Trans.:* 'On the Psychical Mechanism of Hysterical Phenomena: Preliminary Communication', *C.P.*, 1, 24; *Standard Ed.*, 2, 3.]

(1895*d*) With BREUER, J., *Studien über Hysterie*, Vienna, *G.S.*, 1; *G.W.*, 1, 75. Omitting Breuer's contributions. (6, 27, 30, 41)
[*Trans.: Studies on Hysteria, Standard Ed.*, 2; *I.P.L.*, 50. Including Breuer's contributions.]

(1900*a*) *Die Traumdeutung*, Vienna, *G.S.*, 2–3; *G.W.*, 2–3. (xii, xiii, 12–14, 26–28, 37, 41)
[*Trans.: The Interpretation of Dreams*, London and New York, 1955; *Standard Ed.*, 4–5.]

(1905*c*) *Der Witz und seine Beziehung zum Unbewussten*, Vienna. *G.S.*, 9, 5; *G.W.*, 6. (42)
[*Trans.: Jokes and their Relation to the Unconscious*, London, 1960; *Standard Ed.*, 8.]

(1905*d*) *Drei Abhandlungen zur Sexualtheorie*, Vienna. *G.S.*, 5, 3; *G.W.*, 5, 29. (38, 64, 66, 70)
[*Trans.: Three Essays on the Theory of Sexuality*, London, 1949; *Standard Ed.*, 7, 125; *I.P.L.*, 57.]

(1910*i*) 'Die psychogene Sehstörung in psychoanalytischer Auffassung', *G.S.*, 5, 301; *G.W.*, 8, 94. (61)
[*Trans.:* 'The Psycho-Analytic View of Psychogenic Disturbance of Vision', *C.P.*, 2, 105; *Standard Ed.*, 11, 211.]

(1911*b*) 'Formulierungen über die zwei Prinzipien des psychischen Geschehens', *G.S.*, 5, 409; *G.W.*, 8, 230. (xxxi, 7)
[*Trans.:* 'Formulations on the Two Principles of Mental Functioning', *C.P.*, 4, 13; *Standard Ed.*, 12, 215.]

(1914*c*) 'Zur Einführung des Narzissmus', *G.S.*, 6, 155; *G.W.*, 10, 138. (38, 62)
[*Trans.:* 'On Narcissism: an Introduction', *C.P.*, 4, 30; *Standard Ed.*, 14, 69.]

(1914*g*) 'Weitere Ratschläge zur Technik der Psychoanalyse: II Erinnern, Wiederholen und Durcharbeiten', *G.S.*, 6, 109; *G.W.*, 10, 126. (19)
[*Trans.:* 'Recollecting, Repeating and Working Through (Further Recommendations on the Technique of Psycho-Analysis, II)', *C.P.*, 2, 366; *Standard Ed.*, 12, 147.]

(1915*c*) 'Triebe und Triebschicksale', *G.S.*, 5, 443; *G.W.*, 10, 210. (34, 66, 74)

[*Trans.:* 'Instincts and their Vicissitudes', *C.P.*, 4, 60; *Standard Ed.*, 14, 111.]

(1915e) 'Das Unbewusste', *G.S.*, 5, 480; *G.W.*, 10, 264. (3, 26, 31)
[*Trans.:* 'The Unconscious', *C.P.*, 4, 98; *Standard Ed.*, 14, 161.]

(1916–17) *Vorlesungen zur Einführung in die Psychoanalyse*, Vienna. *G.S.*, 7; *G.W.*, 11. (21)
[*Trans.: Introductory Lectures on Psycho-Analysis*, revised ed., London, 1929 (*A General Introduction to Psychoanalysis*, New York, 1935); *Standard Ed.*, 15–16.]

(1917b) 'Eine Kindheitserinnerung aus *Dichtung und Wahrheit*', *G.S.*, 10, 357; *G.W.*, 12, 15. (16)
[*Trans.:* 'A Childhood Recollection from *Dichtung und Wahrheit*', *C.P.*, 4, 357; *Standard Ed.*, 17, 147.]

(1917d) 'Metapsychologische Ergänzung zur Traumlehre', *G.S.*, 5, 520; *G.W.*, 10, 412. (26, 34)
[*Trans.:* 'A Metapsychological Supplement to the Theory of Dreams', *C.P.*, 4, 137; *Standard Ed.*, 15, 219.]

(1919d) Einleitung zu *Zur Psychoanalyse der Kriegsneurosen*, Vienna. *G.S.*, 11, 252; *G.W.*, 12, 321. (10, 38)
[*Trans.:* Introduction to *Psycho-Analysis and the War Neuroses*, London and New York, 1921. *C.P.*, 5, 83; *Standard Ed.*, 17, 207.]

(1919h) 'Das Unheimliche', *G.S.*, 10, 369; *G.W.*, 12, 229.
[*Trans.:* 'The Uncanny', *C.P.*, 4, 368; *Standard Ed.*, 17, 219.]

(1920f) 'Ergänzungen zur Traumlehre' (Abstract of Congress Address), *Int. Z. Psychoan.*, 6, 397.
[*Trans.:* 'Supplements to the Theory of Dreams', *Standard Ed.*, 18, 4; *I.P.L.*, 4, x.]

(1920g) *Jenseits des Lustprinzips*, Vienna. *G.S.*, 6, 191; *G.W.*, 13, 3.
[*Trans.: Beyond the Pleasure Principle*, *Standard Ed.*, 18, 7; *I.P.L.*, 4.]

(1921b) Introduction in English to J. Varendonck's *The Psychology of Day-Dreams*, London; *Standard Ed.*, 18, 271.
[*German Text* (part only): *G.S.*, 11, 264; *G.W.*, 13, 439.]

(1923b) *Das Ich und das Es*, Vienna. *G.S.*, 6, 353; *G.W.*, 13, 237. (20, 62, 65)
[*Trans.: The Ego and the Id*, *Standard Ed.*, 19, 3; *I.P.L.*, 12.]

(1923c [1922]) 'Bemerkungen zur Theorie und Praxis der Traumdeutung', *G.S.*, 3, 305; *G.W.*, 13, 301. (21, 37)
[*Trans.:* 'Remarks on the Theory and Practice of Dream-Interpretation', *C.P.*, 5, 136; *Standard Ed.*, 19, 109.]

(1924c) 'Das ökonomische Problem des Masochismus', *G.S.*, 5, 374; *G.W.*, 13, 371. (5, 6, 7)
[*Trans.*: 'The Economic Problem of Masochism', *C.P.*, 2, 255; *Standard Ed.*, 19, 157.]

(1925a [1924]) 'Notiz über den "Wunderblock" ', *G.S.*, 6, 415; *G.W.*, 14, 3. (27, 32)
[*Trans.*: 'A Note upon the "Mystic Writing-Pad" ', *C.P.*, 5, 175; *Standard Ed.*, 19, 227.]

(1925e [1924]) 'Die Widerstände gegen die Psychoanalyse', *G.S.*, 11, 224; *G.W.*, 14, 99. (60)
[*Trans.*: 'The Resistance to Psycho-Analysis', *C.P.*, 5, 163; *Standard Ed.*, 19, 213.]

(1926d) *Hemmung, Symptom und Angst*, Vienna. *G.S.*, 11, 23; *G.W.*, 14, 113. (11, 20, 34)
[*Trans.*: *Inhibitions, Symptoms and Anxiety, Standard Ed.*, 20, 77; *I.P.L.*, 28.]

(1930a) *Das Unbehagen in der Kultur*, Vienna. *G.S.*, 12, 29; *G.W.*, 14, 421. (66)
[*Trans.*: *Civilization and its Discontents*, London and New York, 1930; *Standard Ed.*, 21, 59.]

(1940d) With BREUER, J., 'Zur Theorie des hysterischen Anfalls', *G.W.*, 17, 9. (6)
[*Trans.*: 'On the Theory of Hysterical Attacks', *C.P.*, 5, 27; *Standard Ed.*, 1.]

(1941a) Brief an Josef Breuer, *G.W.*, 17, 5. (6)
[*Trans.*: A Letter to Josef Breuer, *C.P.*, 5, 25; *Standard Ed.*, 1.]

(1942a) 'Psychopathic Characters on the Stage', *Standard Ed.*, 7, 305. Translation of 'Psychopathische Personen auf der Bühne', which has not been published in German. (17)

(1950a) *Aus den Anfängen der Psychoanalyse*, London. [Includes 'Entwurf einer Psychologie' (1895).] (xxxi, 46, 27–29, 31–34, 77–78)
[*Trans.*: *The Origins of Psycho-Analysis*, London and New York, 1954. (Partly, including 'A Project for a Scientific Psychology', in *Standard Ed.*, 1.)]

(1955c) 'Gutachten über die elektrische Behandlung der Kriegsneurotiker'; German text unpublished. (10)
[*Trans.*: 'Memorandum on the Electrical Treatment of War Neuroses', *Standard Ed.*, 17, 211.]

FREUD, S., FERENCZI, S., and others. (1919) *Zur Psychoanalyse der Kriegsneurosen*, Vienna. (10)

[*Trans.: Psycho-Analysis and the War Neuroses*, London and New York, 1921.]

GOETTE, A. (1883) *Über den Ursprung des Todes*, Hamburg. (56)

HARTMANN, M. (1906) *Tod und Fortpflanzung*, Munich. (56)

JUNG, C. G. (1909) 'Die Bedeutung des Vaters für das Schicksal des Einzelnen', *Jb. psychoanal. psychopath. Forsch.*, 1, 155. (24)
[*Trans.:* 'The Significance of the Father in the Destiny of the Individual', *Collected Papers on Analytical Psychology*, London, 1916, 156.]

LIPSCHÜTZ, A. (1914) *Warum wir sterben*, Stuttgart. (56, 66)

LOW, B. (1920) *Psycho-Analysis*, London. (67)

MARCINOWSKI, J. (1918) 'Die erotischen Quellen der Minderwertigkeitsgefühle', *Z. Sexualwiss.*, 4, 313. (22)

PFEIFER, S. (1919) 'Äusserungen infantil-erotischer Triebe im Spiele', *Imago*, 5, 243. (13)

RANK, O. (1907) *Der Künstler*, Vienna. (66)

RICKMAN, J. (ed.) (1937) *A General Selection from the Works of Sigmund Freud*, London. (xxxi)

SCHOPENHAUER, A. (1851) 'Über die anscheinende Absichtlichkeit im Schicksale des Einzelnen', *Parerga und Paralipomena*, 1 (*Sämtliche Werke*, ed. Hübscher, Leipzig, 1938, 5, 213). (60)

SPIELREIN, S. (1912) 'Die Destruktion als Ursache des Werdens', *Jb. psychoanal. psychopath. Forsch.*, 4, 465. (66)

STÄRCKE, A. (1914) Introduction to Dutch translation of Freud's ' "Civilized" Sexual Morality and Modern Nervous Illness', Leyden. (66)

VARENDONCK, J. (1921) *The Psychology of Day-Dreams*, London.

WEISMANN, A. (1882) *Über die Dauer des Lebens*, Jena. (54)
(1884) *Über Leben und Tod*, Jena. (54–56)
(1892) *Das Keimplasma*, Jena. (54, 67–68)
[*Trans.: The Germ-Plasm*, London, 1893.]

ZIEGLER, K. (1913) 'Menschen- und Weltenwerden', *Neue Jb. klass. Altert.*, 31, 529. (70)

GENERAL INDEX

This index includes the names of non-technical authors. It also includes the names of technical authors where no reference is made in the text to specific works. For references to specific technical works, the Bibliography should be consulted.

Mental apparatus, 5–9, 12, 26,
33–37, 41, 75–76
Mephistopheles (in *Faust*), 51
Migration of birds and fishes,
14
Mother, child's fear of losing,
13–15
Myths, 69–70, 70*n*

Narcissism, 22, 62–65, 71
and physical injury, 38
'of germ-cells', 60
Neuroses (*see also* Obsessional
neurosis;
Transference-neuroses;
Traumatic neuroses; War
neuroses)
sexual aetiology of, 47–49, 63
theory of, 47–48, 60
Neurotics
compared to normal persons,
23
psycho-analysis of, 20–23,
41–43
'Nirvana principle', 67

Object-choice, 60–66, 73*n*
Object-instincts, 73*n*
Oedipus complex, 19, 21–22
Oral phase, 65
Organic
injury, and neurosis, 10–11, 38
life, and the compulsion to
repeat, 43–45, 48–49, 52–53,
71–75

Pain, physical, 34–35
Pan-sexualism, 63
Parental complex, 21*n*
Parents and children, relation
between (*see also* Father;
Mother; Oedipus complex),
21–22
Pcpt. (*see* Perceptual system)

Pcs. (*see* Preconscious system)
Perceptual system, 26–28, 32
Periodicity (*Fliess's* theory of), 54
Perversion, 64–65
Phantasies
wishful, 43
Phobias (*see also* Anxiety), 57
Physical
injury and neurosis, 11, 38
pain, 34–35
Plants, 47, 54
Plato, 69–70, 70*n*
Play of children, 13–17, 24–25,
42
Pleasure principle
dominance of, 3–9, 16–17, 21,
33–42, 67, 75–77
over-ridden by compulsion to
repeat, 13–17, 21–25, 75
relation to principle of
constancy, 5–6
Preconscious system, 20, 40–41
Primary process (*see also* Energy,
psychical, bound and
unbound), 7, 40–41, 75–77
Primitive peoples, superstitious
beliefs of, 53
Principle
constancy, 6, 6*n*, 76
insusceptibility of uncathected
systems, 34*n*
neuronic inertia, 6*n*
'Nirvana', 67
pleasure (*see* Pleasure principle)
reality, 7–8, 21, 41
stability (*Fechner*), 5
Projection, 33
Protective shield against stimuli,
30–37
Protista, 52–59, 66–71
Psycho-analytic technique,
18–22
Psycho-analytic theory, 3
'pan-sexualism' of, 63